DISCA

Redefining the Whole Curriculum for Pupils with Learning Difficulties

To pupils, staff, families and friends, who present us with
a perpetual challenge.

Redefining the Whole Curriculum for Pupils With Learning Difficulties

Judy Sebba,
Richard Byers
& Richard Rose

David Fulton Publishers
London

David Fulton Publishers Ltd
2 Barbon Close, London WC1N 3JX

First published in Great Britain by
David Fulton Publishers 1993

Note: The right of Judy Sebba, Richard Byers and Richard Rose to be identified as the authors of this work has been asserted by them in accordance with the Copyright, Designs and Patents Act 1988.

Copyright © Judy Sebba, Richard Byers, and Richard Rose

British Library Cataloguing in Publication Data

A catalogue record for this book is available from the British Library

ISBN 1-85346-226-8

All rights reserved. No part of this publication may be reproduced, stored in a retrieval system or transmitted, in any form, or by any means, electronic, mechanical, photocopying, recording or otherwise, without the permission of the publishers.

Typeset by ROM Data Corporation Limited, Falmouth, Cornwall, England
Printed in Great Britain by The Cromwell Press Ltd., Melksham, Wilts.

Contents

Acknowledgements

The writing of this book was stimulated by our work on the National Curriculum Development Team (Severe Learning Difficulties) during 1989-91. We continue to work closely with other members of the team and many of them read parts, or all of the manuscript. We are therefore indebted to David Banes, Caroline Coles, Lorraine Cooper, Ann Fergusson, Will Fletcher, Sandra Galloway, Hazel Lawson and Jan Tyne. We are particularly indebted to Dale Lawson for arriving in time to ensure his mother was on maternity leave when we most needed her comments. Constructive suggestions were also provided by a number of other colleagues including Sue Upson, Peter Rushton and John Clarke. We are grateful to Ron Best for permission to quote extensively from his work in chapter five, and to Colleen McLaughlin whose ideas have also informed this chapter.

Finally, the responsibility for the contents in this book is ours and we hope it will motivate teachers and others to question, reflect and ultimately move their practices forward to the benefit of the pupils with whom they work.

Introduction

Aims

The overall aim of this book is to challenge existing assumptions about the curriculum for pupils with learning difficulties. Historically, concepts of 'special educational need' have led to curriculum development that was essentially separate from that relating to all other pupils. They contributed to the development of a range of specific approaches to teaching pupils labelled as 'different'. These methods were tried and less frequently, evaluated, with the debate focusing on the relative effectiveness of each approach in overcoming pupils' problems. Alongside this debate, the content of the curriculum was defined, redefined and streamlined in order to give greater emphasis to the areas considered most essential.

The introduction of a National Curriculum to which all pupils have a legal entitlement has re-focused the debate. The issues now revolve around whether pupils with learning difficulties can, or should, be following a mainstream curriculum. If so, does the current National Curriculum on offer provide a basis for meeting their wide range of individual needs and how can the areas which were seen as crucial in the established curriculum, for example, the therapies, be maintained within the new structure? The 'special' curriculum safeguarded the important contribution made by therapies. The establishment of close working relationships between teachers, therapists and parents will need to be maintained. It is therefore not surprising that at the time of writing, there are still many school staff who consider that the introduction of the National Curriculum threatens the aims of education for pupils seen as having 'special educational needs'.

We suggest in this book that the traditional view of the curriculum for pupils with 'special needs' had an important role in developing our current thinking, but now needs to be challenged. Elsewhere, we have suggested in more detail

(Sebba and Byers, 1992) that the assumptions on which it is based can no longer be defended. While special provision exists, some teachers, schools or increasingly, governing bodies will seize the chance to pass the 'problem' to someone else. Pressure on schools to produce better results may be increasing the tendency to 'pass the buck' through more referrals for statements or requests for school transfer. In doing so, school staff have missed an opportunity, in the words of Hart and Ainscow (1992) to:

> ...learn from the difficulties experienced by some children about the limitations of provision currently made for all pupils.

Hence, curricular changes introduced in order to benefit those experiencing difficulties, will be likely to enhance the learning of all pupils. This requires school staff, in particular teachers, to be more reflective and analytical of their current practice. We are well aware that in general, the current situation gives teachers neither the time nor the confidence to do this.

School staff will need to create the time, commitment and confidence, not only for this reflection and analysis at classroom level but for a more fundamental review of curricular aims and ethos which we suggest in the following chapters. This review of curriculum development will need to remain coupled to the 'real' needs of pupils. The support services provided have tended to be reactive rather than proactive, responding to requests for statements or transfers rather than providing clear criteria of what constitutes appropriate curricula for all. Changes which are taking place at local and national levels provide an opportunity to take a more proactive stance, although it has yet to be seen whether the current national policy changes will be detrimental rather than helpful to pupils experiencing difficulties.

Continuing patterns of curriculum development for pupils wit 'special needs' have led to a narrowing of the curriculum on offer. In the context of mainstream schools, decisions have been made about which areas of the curriculum can be missed in order to focus more specifically on skills seen to be needing extra attention. This has been overcome, to some extent, by the increase in class-based support provided across the curriculum, reflecting whole school policies on 'special educational needs'. However, the presence of an assistant or support teacher brings its own set of potential difficulties which may, for example, reduce the opportunities that particular pupils have to learn cooperatively in groups.

Within schools for pupils with learning difficulties, the curriculum has narrowed as it has been redefined to address independence skills in order to meet those needs perceived as greatest by the staff and parents. Focusing on individual programmes has also led to an over-emphasis on skills in particular areas that lend themselves to clear targets and criteria for success. Activities for which it is more difficult to define outcomes, have been perceived as less important.

The notion of curriculum entitlement for all pupils may offer the opportunity to challenge attempts to segregate pupils who are different. It also challenges narrowing the curriculum and maintaining a fundamental belief that if a pupil does not learn it is because she has a problem which demands remediation through 'special' techniques or a different curricular focus. We now have a basis for providing the same breadth and balance for all pupils and for reanalysing problems which occur to see if the curricular content or delivery could better address the needs of all pupils. The National Curriculum in its current form may not yet represent a complete response but its content is being constantly reviewed and changed. Furthermore, the core and other foundation subjects form only a part of the whole curriculum. Hence, those of us who have much experience of work with pupils who have been designated as having 'special educational needs' have a responsibility to contribute to these changes in order to make the curriculum more appropriate and relevant for all pupils. Throughout this process, the principle of entitlement must be maintained.

It is the purpose of this book to raise issues and provoke practitioners to reconsider the basis of their current practice. We are not providing a textbook on special education based on a comprehensive analysis of the available literature. We are exploring a series of stances which we attempt to explain and discuss in order to encourage professional reflection and development. It is not our ultimate intention that readers necessarily adopt the same positions as we are taking ourselves. Rather, that they use the arguments and discussion to reflect, reconsider and progress. The outcome should be a teacher-owned vision of the curriculum, irrespective of its precise content.

In chapter one we take an historical perspective, recognising the developments that led us to current practice. In chapter two we examine the relationship between the established curriculum, National Curriculum and whole curriculum. In chapter three we consider teaching and learning styles, in particular the role of cross curricular approaches or topic work, individual programmes and group work. In chapter four we look at the wider context of the curriculum, how it is managed through development planning, organisation of staff, timetabling and resources. In chapter five we explore the conceptualisation of personal and social development as a basis for future curriculum development.

Chapter five raises fundamental issues about the ethos of schools and challenges the established power relationships between teachers and pupils. It is also consistent with the view that what constitutes effective practice for pupils with 'special educational needs' is likely to benefit all pupils. Personal and social development is a common educational aim for all pupils and not inconsistent with the existence of a National Curriculum. But we suggest that it does demand a reconsideration of the nature of power and control in all schools. This is the nature of the debate we hope to launch with this book.

Who are we aiming at?

Teachers of pupils with''special educational needs' in any context are the main focus for our work. However, we would hope that classroom assistants, therapists, psychologists, advisory staff and lecturers would all find the perspectives on curriculum of interest and use. Most important, while it is unlikely that any of the pupils we are writing about will read the book, we would hope they could become the main beneficiaries of its content.

Terminology

The text refers throughout to pupils with learning difficulties. We would have preferred to refer to 'pupils who are labelled as having...' or 'pupils deemed to have...' or some other phrase indicating the lottery nature of the system which leads to one pupil being given a label where another similar pupil has a different label or no label. In the interests of readability we have chosen the shorter version of 'pupils with learning difficulties.' However, we remain sceptical about the usefulness of this terminology. This leads us to keep reminding ourselves that labels are based on value judgments, which, however professional, may be misguided. It is an essential component of our position that the label should never be used to justify staff behaviour which threatens the dignity, rights or confidence of the pupils with whom we work. Hence, we adhere to the 'people first' principle throughout the text by referring to 'pupils with...'.

Our own experience has been mainly in schools for pupils with severe learning difficulties. Where the point being made relates specifically to these pupils, we shall refer to them as such. Likewise, we refer to schools for pupils with learning difficulties or mainstream schools when the comments are specific to these contexts. Elsewhere, our limited but significant broader experiences as teachers, parents and governors have been drawn upon to make points which we are confident apply to all pupils.

We refer to''pupils' rather than 'children' since many of the schools catering for pupils with learning difficulties cater for the full age range of 2-19 years. Justifications elsewhere for referring to 'children' stem from views about their developmental status. Central to our position is the notion that pupils who are considered to have learning difficulties retain their rights to independence, dignity, respect, choice and privacy. Hence, by referring to 'pupils', or 'students' where we are specifically addressing older groups, we hope to encourage staff to establish appropriate relationships and contexts.

As a contribution to redressing gender stereotyping of the past, we refer to pupils as 'she' and teachers as 'he'. This is not to deny the clear pattern of staffing in schools for pupils with learning difficulties, in which most teachers and almost all assistants are female but to challenge the assumptions which lie behind it. In keeping with many other writers, we have pluralised the pronouns where possible.

The term ''topic' has been at the centre of the controversy in primary education in recent years. In chapter three we discuss some of the issues surrounding this, and other approaches. Thereafter, we refer to integrated schemes of work which we define and illustrate in chapter three or to cross curricular approaches. We use these terms to describe approaches that combine the most effective features from the teaching styles established in the past.

Finally many of the staff with whom we have worked have found our numerous references to practical examples useful. This book is about issues and ideas. We have included only a few descriptions of practical classroom activities. These are used to illuminate and clarify the points being made. We intend to follow this book with a second volume which provides detailed examples of practice. The debate in the following chapters will seek to provide the rationale for the examples in the second volume.

Chapter One

Setting the Scene

Introduction

The teaching of history is sometimes justified by references to understanding the present in the context of the past. This chapter attempts to describe the context for the debates about curricular content, teaching and learning styles and the management of the curriculum which follow in the subsequent chapters. An understanding of where we are coming from, and of the past and continuing debates may enable current curriculum development to be informed by wisdom rather than intuition or ideology. The historian would no doubt suggest that we might learn from our past mistakes.

We offer below an historical survey which will be brief because some good and comprehensive surveys already exist (e.g. Fagg, 1991; Tilstone, 1991). Our present purpose is to look at the current debate and possible ways forward.

This chapter will suggest both positive aspects of past developments that we might need to protect and develop and negative aspects that we need to continue to challenge. This will set the context for the way in which we attempt to redefine the whole curriculum for students with learning difficulties in the final chapter. Throughout our work we wish to recognise and acknowledge the important contributions made by others in the past while encouraging a reflective and critical approach to current practice. We would wish this to be interpreted as a positive striving for more effective practice rather than a negative dismissal of current work.

Provision for pupils with learning difficulties

Most pupils who are identified as having special educational needs are currently educated in mainstream schools. A relatively small proportion are educated in schools for pupils with learning difficulties (often referred to as the Warnock 2%, from the Warnock report - DES, 1978). Of these, an even smaller proportion, those with severe learning difficulties, were included in the education system for the first time in 1971, following the 1970 Education Act. Hence, curriculum development in this area has a relatively limited history.

Prior to 1971, pupils deemed to have an IQ of less than 50, were assumed to be ineducable and did not receive any kind of instruction. They were cared for in junior training centres in which some teaching of independence skills was targeted. The general ethos emphasised care and 'keeping them happy' and a major purpose of this provision was to give relief to parents. This ethos is still evident in some schools today and has been used, in some instances, as a justification for rejecting the National Curriculum.

The influence of medical models

Throughout this period, the medical model which largely upstaged the genetic model (on which eugenics were based), maintained its stronghold. Pupils were described on the basis of their deficits, with an emphasis on what they could not do as a result of various 'syndromes' and any pupil with a syndrome was assumed to have all the characteristics of that syndrome. This led to stereotypes such as the image of the 'happy, musical mongol'. It is therefore not surprising that we encounter staff who have preconceived notions of pupils' abilities which can provide a justification for their failure to learn. These notions disabled pupils further.

A current example of a label creating further special needs is within the area labelled as 'autism'. Pupils are labelled as 'autistic' provided they display sufficient of the characteristics associated with the condition. These characteristics were originally identified by the medical profession. There is little doubt that many people coming into contact with a person who has been labelled 'autistic' will assume they have, or will develop, all the characteristics associated with the label. The work of Crossley and her colleagues in Australia, described and evaluated by Biklen (Biklen, 1990; Biklen et al, 1991) provides a salutary warning of the dangers of creating low expectations through the process of labelling. Establishing communication with these students required interactions that were supportive and trusting, regarding them as competent and communicating directly to them, never patronizing them. Under these conditions, some students demonstrated literacy skills that had previously been assumed to be unachievable.

The control of junior training centres transferred from health to education in 1970. They thus, officially, became schools but medics and paramedics still made the decisions about who went where and what additional treatment (drug, physiotherapy, etc.) should be made available. Multi-professional work was dominated and meetings were often chaired by the psychiatrist, paediatrician or other medical officer. Even today, it is not uncommon to find therapists deciding when to withdraw pupils for particular work, thereby influencing the timetable, and for schools who do not comply to be threatened with withdrawal of the service.

The influence of psychology on curriculum development

The Influence of Psychometrics

The use of psychometric tests to determine educability has a long history and is an extension of the use of IQ and diagnostic testing to determine school placement, a practice which still exists in some areas. What has been clear for many years is that these procedures are of questionable validity and reliability. These problems are compounded as the degree of disability increases. Hence, there was a period in curriculum development in the 1960s and 1970s which was characterised by training pupils on what were essentially test items. The curriculum tended to be driven by either 'tests' or 'tender loving care'.

The shortcomings were evident. Either we were teaching pupils to perform what were essentially meaningless tasks which they could not generalise, but which bumped up their test performance, or we were teaching them, somewhat misleadingly, to depend upon and trust all adults. The danger of allowing the curriculum to become assessment-led is an issue we are currently facing in relation to the National Curriculum. Teachers are inevitably teaching to the Standard Assessment Tasks (SATs) in response to the pressure created by the publication of test results.

The Influence of Developmental Psychology

The developmental model emerged from both medical and psychological influences. Milestones of development which enable a pupil to be measured directly or indirectly against a 'norm' were used as a basis for developmental checklists. Some of these were based on established paediatric practice (e.g. Sheridan, 1975) while others were specifically designed for assessing pupils with severe learning difficulties (e.g. Gunzberg, 1968) often in an institutional setting. Progress was recorded on a hierarchical scale with a structured path for planning remediation when an individual failed to meet the targets.

The influence of developmental psychology on classroom practice for pupils with learning difficulties was evident. Activities aimed at developing cognitive skills became commonplace. Piagetian-based tasks were introduced and research carried out which compared the performances of pupils with delayed development to those of their 'normally-developing' peers. The development of reasoning skills and perceptual-motor skills generated more exercises and materials. The influence of Frostig (e.g. Frostig and Horne, 1967) and Kephart (e.g. 1971) became apparent in assessment and teaching.

These approaches emphasised the diagnosis and analysis of individual needs and led to teachers preparing individual learning programmes. This was a crucial development in the history of teaching pupils with learning difficulties and continues to influence current practice and debate. The emphasis within this approach on analysis of learning difficulties was compatible with aspects of the behavioural approaches which developed later.

The Influence of Behavioural Psychology

The development of behavioural techniques based on the work of psychologists such as Skinner (e.g. 1966) has had a powerful and lasting influence on the education of pupils with learning difficulties. These techniques became highly influential as a considerable volume of re-search (e.g. Kiernan & Woodford, 1975) demonstrated their effectiveness both in teaching new skills and in reducing problem behaviours. Throughout this research, training in new skills has consistently produced more reliable results than the reduction or elimination of difficult behaviours.

Behavioural strategies such as task analysis and token economies had widespread influence on practice in educational, occupational and residential provision for people with learning difficulties. They were built into general policies as well as individual programmes. The use of individual objectives, task analysis, shaping, chaining, positive and negative reinforcement and punishment became widespread and were paralleled (some would argue, led) by similar developments in the USA (e.g. Mager, 1962). Issues arising from the use of these techniques are further discussed in chapter three.

The development of teaching packages and schemes

The development of specific curricular content material aimed at pupils with learning difficulties has been much less commercially attractive than reading and mathematics schemes aimed at primary schools. Hence, resource development has tended to be class-based or school-based and only occasionally published and distributed more widely (e.g. Rectory Paddock School, 1983).

All of the approaches described above have influenced the development of commercial teaching packages. Particular schemes have become popular, sometimes because they are associated with the approach that is best established at that time. Packages such as Distar (Carnine, 1977), Education of the Developmentally Young (EDY - McBrien & Foxen, 1981), The Behavioural Approaches to Teaching Package (Batpack - Wheldall & Merritt, 1984), Special Needs Action Project (SNAP - Ainscow & Muncey, 1984), Portage (White & Cameron, 1987) and the Derbyshire Language Scheme (Knowles & Masidlover, 1982) all have their advantages and pitfalls. Yet each of them can be seen in part, or in their entirety, in work with pupils with learning difficulties. Teachers are adept at extracting the components from these schemes which appear to be most effective in their particular situation.

These schemes have offered a clear structure for the induction of new staff, training of staff who transferred from the previous, health service run provision and staff transferring from mainstream provision. Some packages (e.g. Batpack; SNAP) have influenced practice in mainstream schools, potentially giving special educational needs a higher priority. Others, (e.g. Portage; Derbyshire) have provided staff in schools for pupils with learning difficulties with a system which appears to offer a clear and rigorous process of determining objectives for learning and monitoring progress. However, Billinge (1988) noted that learning requires much more than adequately planned, recorded and evaluated classroom work. He sees these packages as a denial of the complexities of the learning process.

Some teaching packages such as Portage, do define the curriculum content often through an objectives-based checklist. In general, the packages aimed at those working with pupils with learning difficulties have tended to focus on methods of delivering the curriculum rather than on its content. Historically, the content was determined by selecting the essentials from the curriculum for young children, lowering the demands and arranging teaching to involve shorter periods of concentration. Commercial packages or schemes aimed at mainstream schools have provided a basis for development of specific curricular areas (e.g. mathematics).

In 1984, the DES (1984) proposed that the curriculum for pupils in schools for pupils with learning difficulties be classified under three headings of 'mainstream plus support' , 'modified' and 'developmental'. The first of these describes a curriculum 'comparable' to that in mainstream schools, the second a curriculum 'similar' to that in mainstream schools and the last refers to what was essentially a 'separate' curriculum. The degree to which these categories have been used as a basis for curriculum delivery rather than merely for administrative purposes of statementing and LEA reporting to the DFE (previously the DES), has been questioned by Swann (1992). Currently, staff in schools for pupils with learning difficulties are attempting to identify the future role of the 'developmental' curriculum vis-a-vis the National Curriculum, a point considered further in chapter two.

The current debate

Behavioural approaches have come under considerable attack in recent years particularly because of their potential to be used inappropriately (e.g. Berger, 1982; Wood & Shears 1986). The precision, detailed observation and recording associated with behavioural approaches have led to assumptions regarding its 'objectivity' which have been repeatedly challenged. Teaching is often removed from the natural context, for example, a pupil being removed from a group P.E. activity in order to complete a structured individual physiotherapy programme. There are then problems with skills taught in one context not generalising to other situations. Assumptions are made that what the teacher selects as praise is always reinforcing whereas, publicly praising a shy pupil for example, may increase withdrawal (Berger, 1982).

A major criticism of these approaches has been the lack of opportunities for fostering positive relationships, personal choice and interactions. Berger (1982) has noted that teachers, by virtue of societal expectations and social role have greater power invested in them than that allowed the pupils. Some classroom problems become apparent because pupils' behaviour may challenge this power and the teacher develops the confrontation through attempts to restore the power bias. In other situations, behavioural approaches encourage this imbalance by limiting the role of the pupil in contributing to the process of learning.

The emphasis on completing individual programmes which focus on current priorities has led to an undervaluing of group work and opportunities for collaborative learning. Yet these pupils cannot develop skills in social interaction with their peers if they are taught predominantly in isolation. The first author may have contributed to the promotion of this process through room management schemes (see for example, Sebba, 1988) designed to maximise individual work time.

Some of these criticisms also apply to the indiscriminate use of teaching packages. Staff may adhere to them rigidly even when the content or procedure is not appropriate to the pupil. They often involve pre-determined objectives and teacher directedness (Billinge, 1988). They fail to encourage pupil involvement in negotiated objectives, self review or recording of learning that has taken place and hence restrict the development of autonomy. The focus of teaching is usually upon specific skills and the application of a system sometimes encourages teaching out of context. Furthermore, most of the packages emphasise individual work to the exclusion of group work.

Changes in the philosophy underlying the provision of services for people with disabilities have occurred which further challenge a rigid behavioural basis for teaching. The development of specialist teaching techniques contributed to the evolving special education sub-culture which has isolated staff from their colleagues in mainstream education. The emphasis on the rights of the individual and community integration has contributed to the popularity of more interactive and 'ecological' approaches. Interactive approaches (e.g. Hewett, 1989) stress the process rather than the product and involve the pupils in negotiation of their own goals and activities. Hewett (1989) uses a well established distinction between the 'core' and 'peripheral' curriculum to suggest that interactive play, commonly associated with parent-infant relationships, might replace the skills-based curriculum as the core curriculum for some students.

A detailed observational study of pupils with disabilities in an institution reported by Gleason (1989) demonstrates the value of taking an ecological approach to curriculum development. He found that when pupils with severe disabilities were interacting playfully, they were separated by staff who assumed that they were fighting or unintentionally hurting one another. Observation of the total ecology of these pupils enabled a more meaningful interpretation to be made of their behaviour.

The principle of providing an educational environment that is least restrictive can be realised through an ecological approach. This considers the physical organisation of the environment, groupings of pupils, management of staff and links with other parts of the pupils' ecology such as their home environment. It is consistent with the move from a deficit model, which explained pupil's failure to learn by reference to the characteristics of that pupil, to models which emphasise the role of the teacher, other pupils, school, home and community as interacting variables in determining learning. At a classroom level, Berger (1982) emphasised the importance of assessing all interactions between teacher, pupil and peer group within the context of the classroom, school and community which have an impact on learning.

Conclusion

Objectives-based curriculum models tended to focus heavily on the skills of communication and independence (including mobility as appropriate). Hence, the curriculum for some pupils with special educational needs has tended to become too narrow. While the necessary emphasis on these skills is recognised, providing opportunities across a wider range of the curriculum is consistent with a post-behaviourist view, which suggests that learning outcomes cannot always be pre-determined.

The need to maintain the rigour in planning and record-keeping, which characterised behavioural approaches, while broadening the curriculum, is recognised. Teaching packages should be considered critically, selectively and adaptably. Future approaches need to seek a broad and balanced curriculum content delivered through flexible use of teaching approaches which emphasise the development of pupil autonomy. The following chapters explore this position in more detail.

Chapter Two

Curricular Content

Introduction

The introduction of a National Curriculum might be seen as having eradi-
cated the curricular content debate. A centrally determined curriculum
spelled out in detail by an ever-increasing, weighty set of documents, would
seem to have left little for teachers or schools to determine for themselves.
There are two main indicators that this is not the case. First, since the initial
phase of the introduction of the National Curriculum in 1989, there have
already been substantial revisions and modifications to the content, exemplified through the recent introduction of the revised mathematics and
science Orders. Secondly, the ten subjects (eleven in Wales) of the National
Curriculum were always defined as only part of the whole curriculum.
Major issues arise over what proportion of the whole curriculum should
consist of these subjects for pupils with learning difficulties and what
constitutes the remaining parts of the whole curriculum.

This chapter explores the debate that has arisen about what constitutes an
appropriate curriculum for pupils with learning difficulties. It considers the
definition of the whole curriculum, the role of subject areas within it and
how subjects are themselves defined and have been re-defined in the light
of the National Curriculum. The issues as to which other curricular areas
are included and the role of these areas within the whole curriculum are
discussed. The relationship of these areas to the cross-curricular elements
is also examined. Consideration is given to the challenge the National
Curriculum has provided to the traditional curriculum for pupils with
learning difficulties. In the light of this debate, the definition of entitlement
and its relationship to access, relevance, individual priorities and experiences are reconsidered. In chapter five, the role of personal and social
development as a basis for the whole curriculum is explored.

Definitions of the whole curriculum

In 'Curriculum Guidance 3' (NCC, 1990a) the whole curriculum is defined as:

- the ten subjects of the National Curriculum;
- religious education;
- additional subjects beyond the ten subjects of the National Curriculum;
- an accepted range of cross-curricular elements;
- extra-curricular activities;
- the spirit and ethos of each school;
- the most effective teaching methods;
- efficient and imaginative management of the curriculum and of the school.

Teaching methods are further explored in chapter three and management of the curriculum in chapter four. It is the intention to focus on issues of content in this chapter. Which additional subjects beyond the ten subjects are appropriate for pupils with learning difficulties? Presumably not the examples provided in *Curriculum Guidance 3* of a second language and economics at Key Stage 4. What is the accepted range of cross-curricular elements and 'accepted' by whom? Which extra-curricular activities are appropriate to meeting the curricular needs of pupils with learning difficulties? These questions will be considered below.

Other sources of professional insight into the definition of the whole curriculum can be found. A less formal definition that emphasises the meeting of individual needs and lends itself well to wholefood analogies, is provided by Ashdown et al (1991, p.13) who describe the whole curriculum as:

> a curriculum diet that sustains the whole pupil rather than causing global malnourishment through experiences that fail to give sustenance.

This definition is provided by these authors as an antidote to Wragg's (1990) 'Mad Curriculum Disease' resulting from too much focusing on the subject Orders, or more specifically, the attainment targets, regarded by many school staff working with pupils with learning difficulties as the 'probably, unattainable objectives'. The distinction between a whole curriculum that sustains the whole pupil, presumably involving the meeting of individual needs, academic or otherwise defined, and one largely defined by subject areas and academic achievement, reflects the broader aims of education. Are pupils being educated for the furtherance of society or for the furtherance of themselves? While it is beyond the scope of this book to enter this philosophical debate in any depth, the definition of an appropriate curriculum for pupils with learning difficulties must ultimately be determined by the definition of the purposes of educating them.

What is clear is that the whole curriculum encompasses a much broader range of components than the subjects of the National Curriculum. Consideration is given below as to which components should inhabit this territory.

Redefining the subjects

The definition of the subject areas is less clear than might be assumed from the documents. The debates that have accompanied the process through working party reports, to consultation reports, to draft Orders, to Orders are indicative of the wide-ranging opinions which exist. In each subject, defining the matters, skills and processes which are required to be taught (programmes of study) and the knowledge, skills and understanding which pupils are expected to acquire (attainment targets) has not simply involved acceptance of established descriptions of the subject. For example, interpretations of what constitutes technology or history have been matters of opinion and for debate. Since many of the National Curriculum subjects are not those traditionally well developed in schools for pupils with learning difficulties (or many primary schools), interpretations in relation to these pupils and contexts are largely hypotheses to be tested. Only time will provide evidence of whether the National Curriculum content is the appropriate content to enable pupils to learn the skills they, or society, require.

The need to define appropriate content at the earliest levels in subjects which traditionally focused on more advanced levels has led to much useful curriculum development work and resources for pupils with learning difficulties. This process has been accompanied at all stages by cries of 'tokenism', used to describe practice which distorts the interpretation of a subject in order to attribute an activity to the National Curriculum. For example, a pupil is stated as doing history because they are being given 'old' items to handle, irrespective of whether they are able to grasp conceptually, the difference between old and new items. More commonly, a group is described as undertaking technology when they are asked to make kites and given a template to use for the shape of the kite at the start of the session (the 'here's one I made earlier' syndrome), thus destroying the essential problem-solving feature of the subject.

Useful examples of appropriate activities relating to science, technology, history and geography have been developed for primary schools and schools for pupils with learning difficulties, usually by school staff with a basis in practice (see for examples, East Sussex County Council 1991; Fagg et al,

1990; Mount and Ackerman, 1991). These enable staff to explore and reflect on practice. However, the fundamental question of whether the National Curriculum is an appropriate curriculum remains unchallenged by these publications. They are designed to assist staff to implement what is taken to be the legal requirements for the curriculum.

Professional collaboration between staff with subject specialisms and those with experience in special needs will be needed to explore whether interpretations of each subject into activities are realistic and helpful or tokenistic. Furthermore, monitoring of the curriculum may continue to be carried out by inspectors who often have little or no experience of pupils with learning difficulties. Hence, they will need to explore realistic definitions of their subject areas with experienced school staff in order to provide appropriate interpretations of subject delivery.

Additional subjects and extra-curricular activities

Selection of the subjects required in addition to those of the National Curriculum will need to take into account the current individual needs of the pupils. However, since there are clearly too many items to fit on a weekly or ten-day timetable, careful consideration of priorities and potential overlap will be needed. English may be seen as occurring through all activities and therefore not requiring specific timetabling but how will breadth and balance within English be ensured and recording take place if it is not specifically targeted? These issues are further explored in chapter four which considers management of the curriculum.

Reference to the literature which has informed the teaching of pupils with learning difficulties, reveals a number of models for defining the subject areas to be covered by the curriculum. The history of curriculum development for pupils with learning difficulties as exemplified by writers such as Tansley (e.g. Tansley and Gulliford, 1960) and Brennan (e.g. 1974) has repeatedly reflected the idea that in special education the definitions of the 'core' and 'peripheral' curriculum are reversed. The 'core' curriculum in special education has consisted of what might be seen as the peripheral curriculum in mainstream schools. Hence, staff working with pupils with emotional and behavioural difficulties work from a personal and social development basis which is more usually regarded as the 'peripheral' curriculum in mainstream schools.

If the areas seen as peripheral or extra-curricular in mainstream schools form the main part of the curriculum in schools for pupils with learning difficulties, what constitute the extra-curricular activities in schools for pupils with learning difficulties? Self-help skills such as washing hands, using the toilet, eating with cutlery, putting on and taking off a coat, are skills which in a mainstream school, the pupils are assumed to have previously acquired at home. These have provided a major area of the curriculum for pupils with severe learning difficulties. Activities presented by staff other than teachers such as physiotherapy, speech therapy or aromatherapy are given high priority in some schools. To label these as extra-curricular would be misleading in terms of their perceived importance and the time allocated to them.

Interdisciplinary teamwork between teachers, assistants and therapists is well established in many schools for pupils with learning difficulties. Therapists identify individual priorities that reflect their own professional discipline and may not fit neatly into curricular areas defined by educationalists. The review and redefining of the curriculum must therefore recognise the unique contribution made by therapists to the overall programme for each pupil. This process enables teachers and therapists to continue to benefit from their differing knowledge and experience. Increasing pressures from the National Curriculum must not be allowed to threaten this but should be used to explore the potential relationships further. Establishing effective teamwork is discussed more fully in chapter four.

Experiences which are provided in order to enhance relationships between pupils or between staff and pupils are crucial to personal and social development. Frequently, this is part of the 'hidden curriculum' which may result in it being regarded as less important. It is possible to consider personal and social development within every area of the curriculum but unless this is explicit, there is a danger that it will not be centrally addressed. These issues are further explored in chapter five.

Cross-curricular elements

The cross-curricular elements include the skills, themes and dimensions of the National Curriculum as follows:

Skills	Themes	Dimensions
Numeracy	Economic & industrial understanding	Equal opportunities
Communication	Health education	Life in a multicultural society
Study	Environmental education	
Problem-solving	Citizenship	
Personal & social	Careers education	
Information technology		

The dimensions have always applied equally to work with pupils with learning difficulties although they are further emphasised by learning difficulties itself being an equal opportunities issue. The themes have titles which suggest they are inaccessible but in fact include examples which are generally easier to access than those found in the subject documents. Many of these examples cover activities that have traditionally formed part of the school for pupils with learning difficulties curriculum e.g. washing, shopping, sex education, etc.

The skills are almost a list of areas in a curriculum designed for pupils with learning difficulties. There is clearly scope for seeing these as the 'core' curriculum. However, one of the benefits of the National Curriculum has been to broaden the traditional curriculum in schools for pupils with learning difficulties. *Curriculum Guidance 3* (NCC, 1990a) stresses the importance of fostering these skills across the whole curriculum in a measured and planned way.

The cross-curricular elements provide reassurance that the curriculum should not focus purely on academic subjects. If the raison d'être for educating these pupils is to enable them to become autonomous and independent then their personal and social development will be paramount. This position is argued cogently by other authors such as Ashdown et al (1991).

Entitlement, access, relevance, priority and experience

The Education Reform Act defines the legal entitlement of all pupils to a broadly based, relevant and differentiated curriculum, including the National Curriculum. This was a breakthrough in the history of special education in that, for the first time, the similarities rather than the differences between pupils were being acknowledged. However, as *Curriculum Guidance 2* (NCC, 1989) pointed out, entitlement to the curriculum does not ensure access to it nor progress within it. The legal requirement for pupils to work mainly within the programmes of study associated with the Key Stage defined by their chronological age has been of great concern to parents, school and LEA staff.

If pupils are working predominantly outside the Key Stage indicated by their age they are required to have their statement revised to indicate this modification to the National Curriculum. This is supposedly to ensure accountability, one of the main justifications for introducing the National Curriculum. However, as the Statutory assessment tests are introduced at the later Key Stages, there are likely to be an increasing number of pupils who are working outside their Key Stage and who do not have a statement of special educational needs. Hence, it seems probable that this requirement for modification will create further special needs.

The current authors would prefer to see some professional responsibility transferred back to teachers in relation to this issue. Teachers working with the pupils would be able to determine when to move from the programmes of study in one Key Stage to another and maximum flexibility would exist to do so across subjects, within subjects and for the same pupil from day to day as appropriate. Circular 17/91 (DES, 1991) accompanying the revised orders for mathematics and science appears to allow for greater flexibility than the wording in previous documents. Changes in this area appear to be imminent.

Meanwhile, it is worth considering why the same pupil may need access to more than one Key Stage programme of study simultaneously. In chapter three a detailed discussion of teaching methods is provided. Suffice it to acknowledge here that the last twenty years of special education has been characterised by individualised programming. This has involved school staff in devising precise objectives specifying criteria for achievement for each pupil and organising the classroom to maximise individual teaching time.

At first sight, the National Curriculum appears to be a list of hierarchically ordered, precisely defined objectives, with variable clarity of the success criteria. Hence, staff in schools for pupils with learning difficulties seized the attainment targets as a new checklist and began task analysing each level 1 statement as their training equipped them to do so efficiently. However, they found many of the statements at the higher levels too far out of reach and progress beyond Key Stage 1 difficult.

This frenzy of activity may have satisfied concerned staff that they were doing something about the National Curriculum, but arguably, it had little to do with meeting the needs of the pupils with whom they work. The attainment targets provide the basis for assessment, whether teacher assessment or tests. In most subject areas, it is the programmes of study which should provide the basis for daily planning, teaching and recording. In some subjects, for example history, it is necessary to consider both the programmes of study and the attainment targets beyond Key Stage 1, when they start to diverge. Hence, issues of access, relevance, priority and experience must be considered in general, in relation to the programmes of study.

A useful distinction can be made between 'experience' and 'achievement'. In practice, providing a broad and balanced range of experiences may involve exploration of later Key Stage programmes of study than those from which the individual priorities are drawn. We all like to have the opportunity to experience activities in which we may have little or no pre-skills and no intention of specifically gaining further skills. Many people experiment with sporting or art or craft activities in which they are not particularly proficient and are not striving to become more skilled. They participate in the activities out of curiosity, to seek novelty or for sheer enjoyment. Entitlement and access are assumed and denial of these opportunities would meet with resistance. However, for few of us are these activities the major priorities in our lives.

Hence, pupils should be offered experiences beyond those which ensure progress in areas defined as current individual priorities. This access may involve providing an activity from Key Stage 3 for a group of pupils with diverse needs and interests including those with profound and multiple learning difficulties. Arguably, we cannot predetermine what the pupil may gain from this experience and low expectations have sometimes characterised special education in an unhelpful way. This may be, in part, related to practices in assessment and subsequent diagnosis of the difficulties not being as effective in schools for pupils with learning difficulties or special needs departments as they are assumed to be (Bennett, 1991).

To illustrate some of these issues, consider an activity designed to address the effects of water on the Earth's surface (science, Key Stage 3). This can be successfully presented at a wide range of levels, through, for example, watering plants in the school grounds, observing hard rain on a mud slope compared with on the tarmac path, etc. Some pupils may learn something of this process and hence will achieve within this area of science even if the school staff could not have predicted they would do so prior to the session. Other pupils, may be able to work on current individual priorities within the context of this activity. For one pupil this teaching context might be used to practise wheelchair mobility skills while another is encouraged to produce the signs for 'rain', 'down' and 'on'. Hence, some pupils may achieve science skills, some mobility or communication skills and some nothing at all (but not necessarily predictably so).

The science activity described above may provide a more relevant context for teaching individual priorities from across the curriculum, than that in which many individual programmes have been conducted in the past. Pupils with learning difficulties have traditionally been withdrawn for intensive individual or small group work in areas of priority. The demands of the National Curriculum in terms of breadth of subject coverage make it imperative that these priorities are build into the context of teaching in the class rather than addressed through a pattern of withdrawal.

Some parts of the programmes of study will doubtless cause major problems of access and raise questions of relevance and priority. For example, in the Key Stage 3 science programmes of study pupils are expected to investigate, by observation, experiment and fieldwork, the properties and formation of igneous, metamorphic and sedimentary rocks, and link these to major features and changes on the Earth's surface. Activities in this area would seem less likely to provide an appropriate or relevant context for developing scientific skills, pursuing priorities or even at an experiential level for some pupils.

Hence, an honest and realistic but flexible approach is required. For each pupil an individual curriculum diet (although not necessarily individually delivered) will have to be designed to meet their needs. The National Curriculum in itself provides for individualised curricula for all pupils, however difficult this may be to implement with a class of 30 or more pupils. It is the formal assessment of it which appears to assume all pupils can follow similar procedures.

The precise content of the whole curriculum will continue to vary from one pupil to another and for the same pupil over time in response to changing needs. The proportion of time allocated to activities derived from the traditional developmental curriculum, the National Curriculum or the cross curricular elements will therefore vary. This can be characterised by the three diagrams below, developed from an excellent chapter by Ouvry (1991) on accessing the National Curriculum for pupils with profound and multiple learning difficulties and first published in Sebba and Byers (1992).

In Figure 1, the National Curriculum forms the main part of the pupil's curriculum. This pupil may be in a mainstream school or possibly a school for pupils with moderate learning difficulties or sensory impairments. In this example, the developmental and therapy components play a definite but less substantial role. Perhaps the pupil has a marked visual impairment and requires specific work on conceptual development and mobility arising from this impairment. The cross-curricular elements will be fostered across the whole curriculum and coverage of them will need to be identified in the context of activities arising in subject areas e.g. economic and industrial understanding in the context of a discussion of social history. Sometimes, the themes will themselves provide a teaching context for subject work e.g. work experience in a shop or office involving mathematical skills.

Figure 2 characterises the pupil with profound and multiple learning difficulties whose diet consists largely of the developmental curriculum which will overlap in parts with National Curriculum e.g. sensory work/science. Some specific contribution is likely to be made to this pupil's curriculum, by the National Curriculum e.g. introducing work on 'hot' and 'cold' (science) or work on mazes (maths & geography). In addition, this pupil will need to continue with specific 'therapy' programmes such as physio-

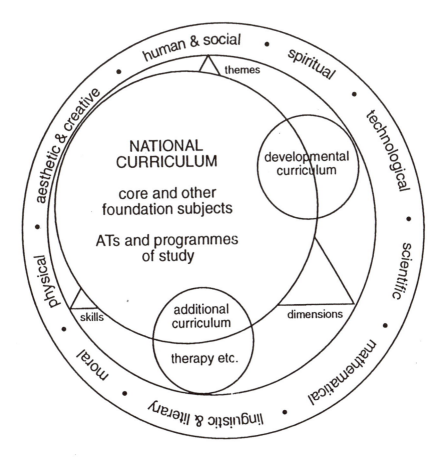

Figure 1:   The whole curriculum 1 (Sebba & Byers, 1992, adapted from Ouvry, 1991)

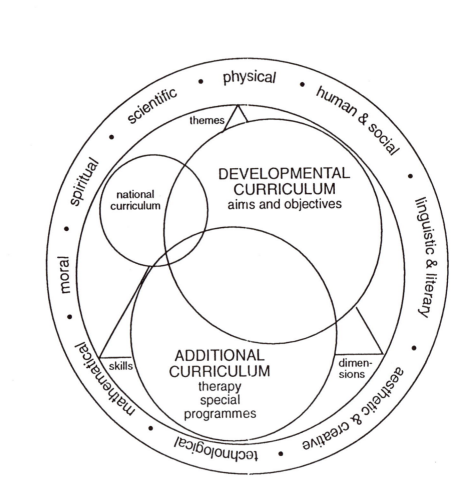

Figure 2:   The whole curriculum 2 (Sebba & Byers, 1992, adapted from Ouvry, 1991)

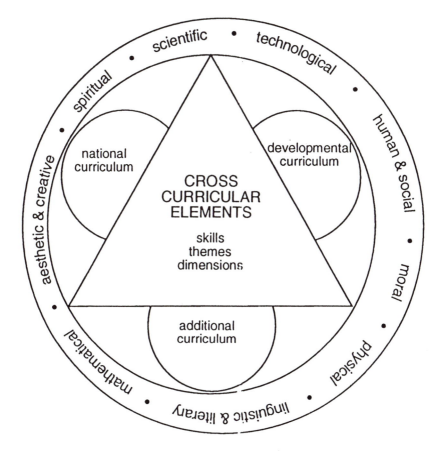

Figure 3:   The whole curriculum 3 (Sebba & Byers, 1992, adapted from Ouvry, 1991)

therapy and feeding but hopefully these will also be integrated into the context of activities arising from National Curriculum or other work. Work developed from the cross-curricular elements will run through all this, for example, the Nature Trail described in *Curriculum Guidance 7* (NCC, 1990e) on environmental education providing a context for practising motor skills prioritised by the physiotherapist, object permanence prioritised from the developmental curriculum and listening skills prioritised from the English programme of study, Key Stage 1.

Figure 3 may be characterised by a pupil with emotional and behavioural difficulties for whom access to the National Curriculum may be sporadic and unpredictable. Further problems can occur when the responsibility for curriculum delivery is shared between two schools or a unit and a school owing to part-time attendance arrangements. The cross-curricular elements covering basic skills eg. numeracy, communication, and most importantly, social and personal development, and themes relevant to the immediate environment e.g. citizenship, are likely to be a major basis on which to hang the rest of the curriculum. In chapter five, we explore the possible justification for using personal and social development as a basis of the curriculum for many pupils with learning difficulties not just those whose behaviour patterns demand it.

Conclusion

This chapter has demonstrated the need to review curriculum content for pupils with learning difficulties. The definition of the whole curriculum and consideration of each of its component parts provides a basis for a realistic and flexible approach to implementing the National Curriculum. As the National Curriculum continues to evolve, hopefully, with increasing relevance for pupils with learning difficulties, and teachers become more familiar with it, the role of the developmental curriculum will diminish. There is little doubt that the demands of time will make it essential to reconsider current provision. Chapter four describes the role of curricular auditing in this process. Changes in content inevitably require changes in teaching methods. The next chapter considers these.

Chapter Three

Teaching Approaches and Learning Styles

Introduction

In this chapter we will argue that the effective implementation of the whole curriculum for pupils with learning difficulties demands the considered deployment of a wide range of approaches to teaching and the deliberate cultivation among pupils of a similarly diverse array of learning styles. The first section of the chapter re-examines the behaviourist tradition and its implications in terms of teaching approaches and learning styles. It notes that the effects of these developments have been both positive and negative. The chapter then discusses integrated approaches to curriculum delivery within the core and other foundation subjects of the National Curriculum and the merits of a balanced variety of teaching approaches.

Finally in this chapter we discuss learning styles and some of the ways in which staff working among pupils with learning difficulties can structure activities in order to facilitate pupil problem solving and co-operative group work. The chapter offers a brief review of the research into group work and shows the relevance of certain aspects of mainstream practice to the teaching of pupils with learning difficulties. We will not seek to minimise the challenge which these shifts in approach represent. Issues concerning pupil groupings and the need for effective differentiation will be addressed. We also suggest methods for developing group work which can inform the planning and preparation of learning activities where school staff wish to extend the range of teaching approaches and learning styles they offer.

The behavioural legacy

Adherents of the behavioural approach to teaching identify three major suppositions which lie behind the methodology (Farrell, McBrien and Foxen, 1992). The first of these concerns the nature of learning itself. Behaviourists argue that learning is a process whereby pupils acquire, or are encouraged to acquire, new or modified behaviours. The model is elaborated by the concept of setting conditions, whereby the antecedents of behaviour and its consequences are considered alongside the behaviour itself. Success is determined by the rate at which the actions of the teacher change or modify observable, externally verifiable skills or competencies in the pupil. It was this version of behavioural methodology which served to underpin much of the early work of schools for pupils with severe learning difficulties.

The second major supposition, which follows from the first, is that teachers, in order to be effective, need to prescribe clear objectives for learners. A neat cyclical process is proposed whereby teachers establish and maintain control over the learning process. Teachers assess learners; set objectives which describe, in terms of observable behaviours, the learners' next steps on the learning ladder; and make records, on the basis of new assessments, of progress measured against performance criteria which were teacher-defined in the first place. In setting objectives teachers may draw inspiration from criterion-referenced checklists. They may also task analyse those skills which seem to be too big to be learned all in one go, so that they become subdivided into a plethora of sub-skills. In this sense, the teaching systems adopted by many schools for pupils with learning difficulties not only encouraged teachers to be prescriptive but also resulted in assessment procedures driving both curriculum content and curriculum delivery.

Thirdly, behaviourism has a great deal to say about teaching techniques. This phraseology is perhaps itself instructive. It pre-empts any discussion about teaching methods. It assumes that there is only one way to conceptualise teaching and that teaching is a technical exercise or a precise science. Basic behaviourist theory suggests that if the right teaching techniques, backward chaining, shaping, modelling, prompting and so on, are applied to an accurately assessed learning situation and directed towards a carefully prescribed objective, then learning will occur and behaviour will change.

Where behaviour does not change, teachers are urged to re-examine the technical detail. Perhaps the initial assessment was not accurate. Perhaps the objective was too distant. Perhaps the rewards selected or the teaching techniques employed were not the most appropriate. In other words, failure to effect change does not indicate a failure of the methodology but simply a failure in its application.

Teacher dissatisfaction

Looking back to the late 1970s (see chapter one), teachers in the new schools for pupils with severe learning difficulties found behaviourism extremely useful. It encouraged a rigorous approach to record keeping. It provided a clear goal-setting structure so that teachers knew exactly where they were heading with each pupil. And pupils did make progress. At least, they made progress quite spectacularly in some areas (self-help skills or motor skills always provided the best examples) but noticeably not in others.

Such anomalies were not necessarily seen as a challenge to structured behavioural methodology. Problems occurred, behaviourists argued, because teachers were not being subtle enough in their application of technique – not setting objectives precisely enough, not task-analysing in enough detail, not selecting exactly the right rewards. Teachers were driven to devise ever more detailed teaching programmes. Elaborately structured ways of teaching language skills and social skills were designed and revised and redesigned. Checklists and charts grew in complexity and multiplied. But there were still some things, such as learning to communicate, that continued to present difficulties. Teachers were left wondering how this could be so. After all, the claim was that behaviourism told teachers all they needed to know about teaching and learning.

Or did it? Many teachers, through the 1980s, began to question the supremacy of structured behavioural techniques and to suggest that, far from being the only way to conceptualise the teaching and learning process, behaviourism represented simply one view of a complex phenomenon. Taking their cue from mainstream education, teachers of pupils with learning difficulties began to see their task in ways other than that defined for them by psychologists. They began to sense that behaviourism was not the only way to plan thoroughly or to structure teaching so that learning might take place. There was a sense indeed that the acquisition of new skills did not represent the sole aim of education.

Criticisms of behaviourism began to take a number of different forms, some of which were discussed in chapter two. Teachers challenged the wisdom of applying behavioural techniques to all forms of learning. It seemed that the group activities which were being offered in schools for pupils with learning difficulties were devalued because they did not appear to address those individual priorities identified within the behavioural structure. The question arose as to whether such activities were therefore educationally insignificant or whether behaviourism itself might, after all, offer an inadequate educational model. If aesthetic appreciation or social interaction did not conform to the model, should they be dropped from the timetable or should a methodology be sought which could facilitate their full integration into the curriculum?

Teachers also began to look carefully at checklists and to wonder whether they might almost be creating as many problems as they were solving. Checklists were essentially designed as tools for assessment, yet they were being used to define the curriculum. The identification of individual needs, a worthy enough aim in itself, was being reduced, in its crudest form, to a formula which involved assessing pupils to the point of failure against a checklist before selecting the next checklist items in the sequence as 'targets'.

Often the checklists themselves seemed to carve up the learning process into arbitrary categories, separating skills and concepts which might have been seen more productively as being connected. Even where teachers were genuinely confident of the line of demarcation between, for instance, 'cognitive' and 'language' skills, these skills were then task analysed and taught to pupils in discrete morsels. Frequently, little attempt was made to allow pupils to see the purpose behind the learning of these sub-skills, perhaps because it was assumed that they could not understand. Instead the sub-skills were taught out of context, during precisely structured one-to-one sessions. Access to any overview which might make sense of the fragments was restricted to the teacher. Teachers began to sense that behavioural techniques might be able to give pupils new skills, or parts of skills, but that they were failing to provide understanding. The old adage that the driver does not need to understand the theory of internal combustion in order to drive the car may be true, but usually drivers do have a sense that a car is a form of transport, that it is intended for taking people to new places, and that there is a relationship between gear change and acceleration.

The national curriculum

All of this criticism seemed to suggest that a reliance upon behaviourism was creating a fragmented learning experience for pupils. The comments of Her Majesty's Inspectorate (e.g. DES, 1989a and 1989b) also suggested that the curriculum in some schools for pupils with learning difficulties had become narrow and restrictive. Pupils were learning how to do certain things without access to a sense of why. They were being offered skills but denied knowledge. Once the autocracy of behavioural thought had been challenged at this fundamental level, other criticisms followed. Recently there has been a tendency for attitudes to become polarised into either the behavioural or the interactive approaches. Doubtless this discussion has an important part to play in the process of change, but it is not the intention of this chapter simply to engage with an already well-rehearsed debate.

The issue is not whether this or that teaching method is best, but whether any single methodology can, on its own, meet all the learning requirements of any group of pupils. The argument is not about whether structured behavioural approaches work (clearly, under certain circumstances, they do) but about whether they should be seen as the only way to teach. This chapter will suggest that a balanced variety of teaching approaches and learning styles is necessary in attempting to promote the balanced development of pupils.

The introduction of the National Curriculum has encouraged many schools to re-examine not only the content of their curricula but also the ways in which teaching is carried out. It is true that initially some schools for pupils with learning difficulties responded, in the only way they felt they could, by seizing upon the statements of attainment as offering an opportunity for some familiar task analysis. Extended attainment target checklists were produced in many schools and the attempt was made to absorb the National Curriculum into the behaviourist scheme of things. It is quite possible that the task analysis of statements of attainment has, in many instances, been useful and provided new insights into routes to attainment for many pupils. However, it cannot be considered a complete response to the National Curriculum.

The programmes of study describe processes as well as outcomes, acknowledging those internal acts of cognition whereby pupils gain knowledge and understanding as well as skills and competencies. They lead towards assessment opportunities but are not defined by them. Further, though they may be seen as prescriptive in terms of subject content, the programmes of study require, at times, a different view of the power relationship between teacher and learner than that implied by behavioural methods. They reflect a discovery-based, investigative, problem-solving vision of education. They also reveal a degree of overlap and interdependence between the subjects. These characteristics encouraged some teachers to begin to think about alternative ways of delivering the National Curriculum and an interest in thematic or topic approaches, which was beginning to emerge prior to the National Curriculum, was encouraged in schools for pupils with learning difficulties.

The topic approach

The topic approach has a long and varied history in mainstream primary education (Conner, 1988). It may be the differences in interpretation and application that have contributed to the controversy surrounding it. A full critique of the topic approach is given elsewhere (Byers, 1990). Its role however, continues to be acknowledged. The recent discussion paper on *Curriculum Organisation and Classroom Practice in Primary Schools* (Alexander, Rose and Woodhead, 1992), for instance, argues for 'an appropriate balance of subject and carefully focused topic work' and states that 'the subject-focused topic, in particular, offers an efficient way forward' in interpreting the programmes of study of the National Curriculum.

Teachers in mainstream schools have, since the 1960s, seen the topic approach as having a number of positive features. It can help to ensure cohesion in a curriculum which has been broken down into subject categories. It can indicate ways in which ideas and concepts come together and make sense from a number of different directions at once. Topics can capitalise upon these natural connections and emphasise the relationships between subjects and between skills and knowledge learned in school and those learned in 'the real world'. For teachers who have become frustrated with the separate, narrow, linear learning routes suggested by checklists and who feel dissatisfied with the kind of fragmented, out of context skills training which has characterised behaviourist methodology, this aspect of teaching by topics may seem particularly attractive.

Further, the topic approach is one of many that require pupils to be active learners. Topics had their heyday in times when methods of encouraging discovery learning were most in favour. It was argued then that pupils should engage their natural inquisitiveness and learn through exploration, enquiry and creative thought. Topics were seen as one important way of developing this level of pupil participation in the learning process. The philosophy which lies behind many of the activities outlined in the programmes of study for National Curriculum subjects at Key Stage 1 builds on this heritage. Words such as 'investigate', 'explore', 'experience' and 'find out about' are used frequently in the Key Stage 1 programmes of study, emphasising the active role which pupils are expected to play in the learning processes relating to all the subjects.

The technology Order provides the most dramatic evidence in support of the claim that the National Curriculum promotes pupil participation. The whole of the programme of study at Key Stage 1 can be seen as a description of a problem solving curriculum, although, according to HMI (DES, 1992), this aspect is not well-implemented in primary schools. Fostering the ability to solve problems, independently and collaboratively, is now seen by some as one of the most useful contributions which schools can make in seeking to promote pupil autonomy. Confidence is required when applying skills in new situations and taking risks. Honest evaluation demands objectivity and robust self-esteem if setbacks and difficulties are to be seen as opportunities to explore failure and attempt new solutions.

In summary, topics demonstrate the relevance and interdependency of subject content while permitting the possibility of active pupil participation in the learning process. A further advantage lies in the opportunities they create for group work and pupil collaboration. Topics were always seen as requiring pupils to work both on their own and in groups, demanding social behaviour, negotiation and teamwork. Again, the programmes of study for the National Curriculum at Key Stage 1 require similar initiatives. Team work and the negotiation of roles within a team form an explicit part of the technology curriculum; the science Order refers to group activity and pupils responding to one another's ideas; the English Order is full of references to group work, group discussion and collaboration. Strategies for promoting group work in schools for pupils with learning difficulties are discussed in detail in the latter part of this chapter. For the present, it is enough to note that a clear link exists between the philosophy of topic work and the expressed intentions of the National Curriculum.

Complementary aspects of the behavioural and topic approaches

The topic approach cannot provide a complete response to National Curriculum implementation. There will continue to be a need for pupils to learn basic skills and competencies individually and in whole class lessons. But providing balance and variety in implementing the National Curriculum will mean taking account of issues such as integrated subject planning, active pupil involvement, learning through problem solving and collaborative group activity.

Happily, looking at teaching in these kinds of ways will also neatly complement the behavioural approach and go some way towards counterbalancing the shortcomings discussed at the beginning of this chapter. Where behaviourism follows checklists of separate, hierarchically-sequenced skills, the topic approach seeks the intentional, creative integration of subjects. Where behaviourism fragments and isolates learning, the topic approach provides contexts geared to real life and pupil interest in which skills may be practised and generalised. Where behaviourism is teacher dominated and prescriptive, the topic approach encourages pupil participation and self-directed learning. Where behaviourism focuses upon skill acquisition in tightly structured one-to-one teaching situations, the topic approach allows pupils to take a collaborative, problem solving, exploratory route to new knowledge and understanding.

At the same time, the topic approach has itself been criticised for promoting vague, undifferentiated learning experiences which lack links with previous activities in terms of continuity and progression and which tend not to be accurately assessed (Eggleston, 1980; Thomas 1982). It is clear that systematic organisation, ensuring differentiation, continuity and progression, and thorough assessment and record keeping practices are precisely the strengths of behaviourist methodology. It would seem that there is a real possibility here for having the best of both worlds.

This may seem encouraging in theory, but difficult to achieve in practice. Clearly new and unfamiliar ways of working will be required of teachers and of pupils. However, many teachers in schools for pupils with learning difficulties are already meeting this challenge and were seeking diversification in terms of content and methodology even before the onset of the Education Reform Act. The National Curriculum simply provides the opportunity to conduct a long-overdue review and to implement some long looked for innovations. In some schools this process is well advanced.

Integrated schemes of work

The strategy of devising integrated schemes of work, described and exemplified elsewhere (Byers, 1990; Sebba et al, 1991; NCC, 1992a), has provided one way forward. Hence, throughout the rest of this book we refer either to integrated schemes of work or cross-curricular approaches. In essence, this way of working seeks to combine the most constructive features of the topic approach with the rigour, structure and attention to detail which characterises objectives based teaching. It represents one way of mapping individual learning routes through an integrated curriculum and of pursuing individual skills in the context of meaningful, relevant group activity. It encourages pupils to take more responsibility for their own learning while allowing the teacher to maintain a clear view of intentions and outcomes.

Let us look at one small example of how this might work in practice. Suppose that the physiotherapist has identified a need for Jenny, a pupil with a number of physical and sensory difficulties, to maintain and develop movement and extension in her arms. Behavioural methodology might suggest that the teacher completes an activity chart for Jenny with the objective: 'Jenny will stretch her arms out in front of her, reaching at least 45 centimetres, ten times a day.' Under a behaviourist regime, this objective may have been achieved by placing Jenny across a foam wedge and exhorting her to 'stretch out, Jenny. Good girl - a bit further. O.K. relax. Now let's do it again. Come on Jenny - stretch.' At the end of each successful stretch, Jenny may have been given a reward in the form of a twenty second burst of her favourite music and, at the end of her one-to-one session, a relaxing swing in the hammock after working so hard. Jenny has completed her task, working individually with a member of staff, and has been rewarded for her success. Perhaps next term the teacher will decide to move Jenny on and get her to reach a full 60 centimetres at each stretch.

There are problems with this. Jenny is working on her own. The activity is isolated and isolating. It is not meaningfully connected to Jenny's experience as a whole person and it does not offer Jenny any contact with her peers. The activity is not self-initiated nor does it offer any intrinsic motivation. Jenny's teacher has offered her no idea of why she is being required to stretch. She has no access to the purpose of this activity other than the realisation, perhaps, that she gets to do something she likes if she tries hard enough. There is no opportunity for Jenny to evaluate the activity or her own performance within it. It is a productive activity for the teacher, who is pursuing one of Jenny's agreed objectives and recording positive results, but for Jenny it is meaningless and repetitive.

The activity could be improved. The teacher could motivate Jenny by giving the stretching action an intrinsically rewarding purpose. Jenny could be encouraged to reach for her biscuit at break time. A contact switch could be attached to a timer on the cassette player so that Jenny gets a burst of music every time she reaches out from her wedge to press the switch. Jenny could be encouraged to reach out and touch people's noses, hair or ears while learning words for parts of the face. These might be seen as more creative ways to pursue Jenny's objective. The activities are purposeful and intrinsically motivating. They may engage Jenny's interest more successfully than the arid stretching for stretching's sake. They may combine several of Jenny's objectives in one complex activity. But Jenny is still working alone and she is still unable to affect the direction which her learning takes.

Suppose now that Jenny is part of a class of pupils with diverse needs engaged in group activity relating to the National Curriculum. Perhaps the class are to measure objects using printed hand spans. Jenny could be encouraged to reach out from her wedge and put her hand print, in the colour of her choice, where she wants it on the paper. Perhaps the class have made rolling toys and wish to find out which one rolls the furthest. The toys could be rolled from Jenny's wedge. Jenny could be given the physical responsibility of the task of measuring how far they go, whether she grasps the mathematical concepts or not. Which ones can Jenny reach? Which one went furthest beyond Jenny's reach? If Jenny really stretches, can she get that one?

Perhaps, on another occasion, a variety of animals are brought into the classroom in order to allow the pupils to 'measure a pet'. Jenny might be motivated enough to want to reach out herself from her chair in order to stroke the rabbit's fur or to feel the smoothness of the snake. If she cannot reach, can she solve this problem for herself before a member of staff steps in to solve it for her? Can she shuffle her chair nearer to the table or indicate to one of her peers that she would like to be pushed nearer? Will she, perhaps, pick up the piece of lettuce and reach out to offer it to the tortoise, indicating that she understands something about the 'variety of plant and animal life' and about animals' needs and the care they require (science, programme of study, Key Stage 1)?

In all these examples, Jenny is part of a group engaged in activities relating to an integrated scheme of work about 'measuring'. The activities bring together the subject content from a number of different National Curriculum Key Stage 1 programmes of study. Jenny is involved in activities relevant to mathematics (non-standard measures) and to technology (evaluating wheeled toys) as well as to science (as has been indicated above) irrespective of whether she has achieved in these subject areas or only in her priority areas (for example, stretching her arms). She has the chance to direct some of her own learning opportunities; to become fully involved with meaningful activity and to engage in the process of evaluation; to make discoveries through her own explorations and investigations and to solve her own problems when they occur.

In each case Jenny is able to work towards maintaining and developing movement and extension in her arms and the teacher has the opportunity to ensure that Jenny practises this skill regularly and that the outcomes are observed and recorded. However, Jenny pursues this objective, through self-initiated activity, in meaningful contexts. Jenny has access to the purposes which give rise to the activities and she is willingly involved. Because there is a reason for reaching and stretching which she perceives, which she may understand and which motivates her, Jenny practises and even generalises the skill which originated as a physiotherapy objective. The sterile pursuit of a closed target competency has been remade as a series of challenging educational encounters, rich in possibilities.

Hence, traditional behavioural approaches tended to stress the need for Jenny's objectives to be addressed in a one-to-one context, whereas the introduction of a greater variety of learning contexts has included some group work. Above all else, Jenny's one-to-one teaching context gave her no access to the purpose or meaning of the activity involved. Individual skills can be taught through one-to-one or group work, in a context in which the pupil is given access to the purpose and meaning of the activity. It is the development of individual skills within group work to which we will now turn.

The role of group work

We would not wish to deny the importance of addressing individuals needs, and there is no reason to suppose that a cross-curricular approach should preclude the addressing of these needs. There are, however, times when in order to promote new skills and experiences, or to introduce new concepts, teachers may wish to focus upon one particular curricular area, making this explicit to the pupils.

For example, let us take a school in which the scheme of work for the term focuses on woodlands. Staff have planned a range of activities which include investigating the commercial uses of wood, mapping a small local woodland, surveying types of trees, recording the creatures which live in the wood, art and craft activities using natural materials collected from the wood, and so on. One afternoon is planned when pupils will search for and examine insects and other small creatures in the wood. The teacher plans that this visit to the wood should form the basis of a week's lessons which will include work from several curricular areas including science, mathematics and art. Before embarking upon this woodland visit, the teacher wants to ensure that as many pupils as possible can use pooters for collecting insects, bug boxes and hand lenses.

In order to facilitate this, he plans one lesson which is intended to teach the use of these pieces of scientific apparatus. He devises a number of games, including one wherein pupils compete to see who can pick up the greatest number of cake decoration balls with a pooter in two minutes. Pupils record their results using a variety of charts in order to gain a greater understanding of the various methods of recording data. This lesson has a skills based scientific focus, and it will have prepared pupils for the use of the apparatus which will enable them to work more effectively in the woodland. This will save considerable time for the teacher who wants to maximise use of the woodland visit for the collection and examination of insects and other small creatures. The concentration upon skills, in this instance, is an important means of ensuring that the group visit to the woods will work more effectively.

Thinking back to the critique of the skills-orientated tuition which Jenny received in pursuit of behavioural objectives in the previous example, it is important to note that the pupils in the activity described here have access to the purpose of learning to use scientific apparatus. The focus of the scheme of work for this term (woodlands) has been shared with them, as has the purpose of visiting the woods. They may therefore understand that they are learning to use pooters, bug boxes and hand lenses because they will need these skills during their collecting expedition. New skills are being given meaning in the context of a broader set of experiences. Furthermore, the woodlands scheme of work ensures that the skills to be practised are relevant to the pursuit of a wider spectrum of learning intentions, so that pupils develop not only new skills, but also new knowledge, understanding and attitudes.

Whilst accepting that individual teaching will always have a place in the education of all children, teachers need to be realistic about the practicalities of offering individual instruction as more than a small part of their teaching time. The reality of most classroom situations is that the time available for individual instruction is very limited, and the sizes of primary school classes have virtually ruled this out. Issues always arise such as, whilst I work with this pupil how do I guarantee the quality of what is happening with the rest of the class? Similarly, there are problems of time management if each pupil in a class is to receive adequate individual attention during the day at times which will allow for both teacher and pupil optimal performance. This problem has been particularly emphasised in classes which include pupils with profound and multiple learning difficulties.

Some teachers have been adept at devising 'holding activities' for pupils which they hope will provide some stimulation to pupils whilst they work intensively with another individual. The validity of this procedure, other than as a relief for teacher conscience must be questioned. The difficulties experienced when working with pupils with profound and multiple learning difficulties can often be intensified when individual instruction demands more than one adult to work with a pupil, as can often be the case, for example, in implementing a physiotherapy programme. Undoubtedly, the need to maintain a relatively high level of individual teaching, particularly for pupils with profound and multiple learning difficulties, will remain. The notions that these pupils cannot be involved in collaborative learning or that group work is less effective in promoting learning, are however, false ones (e.g. Johnson and Johnson, 1982; Rose, 1991).

Whilst there are difficulties which teachers will need to overcome if their lessons are to be truly inclusive, it is essential to begin from the premise that all pupils, regardless of need, have a right to participate in education alongside their peers. An understanding of the needs of individual pupils must combine with an analysis of lesson content, intended outcomes and group dynamics if group work is to prove effective.

Learning is essentially a social activity. How often do we hear clichés about the purpose of education being to prepare pupils for their place in society? The special education movement itself has been promoting the need for acceptance of all pupils in society, no matter how great their disability. Many education authorities have policies with a declared intention of increasing integration. If these ideals are to be achieved, all pupils, including those with severe learning difficulties or emotional and behavioural problems, must develop the skills essential to function in social settings.

Group work, rather than individual instruction has a far greater role to play here. Teachers must, however, accept that collaboration and successful interaction between pupils is in its own right a valid teaching aim.

A shift in emphasis away from individual instruction, and towards more group based activity should not be regarded as a denial of the attention which individuals require and deserve. The value of developing effective social interaction in the learning process can easily be underestimated, and can, as Hart (1992, p.12) has emphasised provide the teacher with even greater opportunities to address the needs of individual pupils:

> Social interaction not only creates opportunities for children to formulate their ideas through talk, to share ideas and resources, to do in cooperation with others activities which they would not yet do alone. It also encourages mutual support which becomes self sustaining, so that the teacher is able to spend more time with individuals or groups, helping to extend and develop their learning.

As stated earlier in this chapter, teachers have become increasingly aware of the difficulties of addressing individual needs, and have begun to examine classroom management to assist with developing group teaching for their pupils. Some schools have moved towards activity based groupings of pupils with similar needs, for example, grouping ambulant pupils from several classes together to make a compatible P.E. group. Others have developed curricular materials designed to promote working in group situations which take full account of individual needs and abilities and promote interaction (Newman and Rose, 1990).

Some schools have found it necessary to vary the groups in which pupils work in order to provide good role models for language, or behaviour. The likelihood is that most pupils will require a variety of group types and compositions. There can, however, be no doubt, that to move forwards to more effective group work requires a radical shift in thinking. For many pupils with severe learning difficulties who have been used to having things done for them, or in some instances done to them, the required move can be seen as being :

from PASSIVE RECIPIENT -----to-----ACTIVE PARTICIPANT

In other words, more classroom activity needs to be either pupil initiated, or teacher/pupil negotiated. Examples of teachers using the demonstration model of teaching in, for example, cookery lessons with pupils with profound and multiple learning difficulties are still common, and in some schools constitute the norm. Here, the teacher sits the pupils around whilst he prepares food, occasionally involving the pupils in tasting or smelling in the hope that some form of educational stimulation will occur. In this instance, which could be seen almost as a form of educational osmosis

40

theory, the pupil is very much a PASSIVE RECIPIENT, and in some instances it is doubtful that they are in fact receiving any useful stimulation or instruction. A more active approach might, for example, involve the pupil in selecting the food.

Such an approach is difficult to assess, and in many instances isolates pupils from all but the adult working directly with them. With this approach, the demands on involving pupils fully in the activity, and cooperatively with classmates can at times be non existent. This is not intended to be critical of teachers, many of whom have had little or no training in the development of collaborative learning. It is, however, one way of indicating that if learning is to take place we need to examine carefully our classroom groupings, and to be more critical of teaching approaches and content.

Grouping and group work

This raises the major issue of distinguishing GROUPING from GROUP WORK, a subject which has received considerable attention. Tann (1988, p.155), for example, makes an important distinction here between:

GROUPING - a system of arranging children into smaller than class size units,

and

GROUP WORK - providing opportunities for children to work together, in a collaborative fashion, on a shared task.

Grouping of pupils is a relatively simple procedure. If, however, it is to promote good learning through group work, it demands considerable thought and preparation. Indeed, Bennett et al (1984) claim that in many instances, the only significant moves following the recommendations of HMI (DES, 1980a) to increase collaborative learning, was a change in classroom seating arrangements. There is a real danger in assuming that when pupils are physically arranged in groups effective group work will take place. It is perfectly possible and quite common, for four pupils to be seated together at a table, but for no interaction to occur.
McCall (1983, p.14) further argues that:

Without useful thought and structuring, small group experience can be unsatisfying for both pupil and teacher, and some small groups can remain a collection of individual learners.

This is certainly a danger in groups of pupils in which diversity of skills and need can exacerbate problems of appropriate grouping. The belief that placing pupils in one group or class will serve to meet all of their needs can often be a false one. It may well be that a group which functions well, and

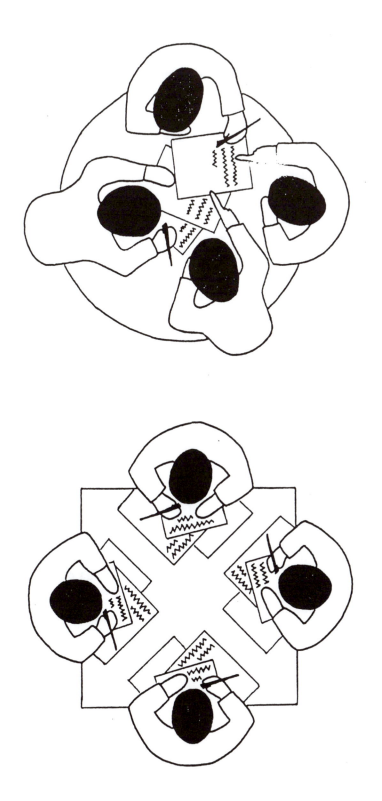

Figure 4: Grouping and group work

allows all pupils to perform well in one situation may be a totally incompatible group in another. When working with groups of pupils whose needs are diverse, problems of differentiation are bound to exist. Bad planning of groups will serve only to increase these problems.

There is certainly a wealth of evidence to suggest that working in small groups, particularly when these groups are focused specifically on a given task, is an effective way to promote learning (e.g. Swing and Peterson, 1982). A major concern however, must be the structure and composition of groups. Swing and Peterson (1982) found that students of low ability functioned well in tasks tackled by mixed ability groups. High ability students also functioned well, though the average ability student seemed to gain least.

Promoting effective group work

Slavin (1987) identified three features of group work which he regarded as essential for success:

(1) Reward - this could simply be the achievement of the set task, or could be something more tangible.
(2) Individual accountability - team success depends upon all individual members achieving their part of the task.
(3) Equal opportunities for success - students all have a role to play, and should contribute to the group by improving upon past performance. This feature, argues Slavin, ensures that high, average and low achievers are all challenged, and that everyone's contribution is valued and forms the basis for what would today be regarded as effective differentiation.

Clearly, an issue which must be addressed concerns the structure of groups if group work is to be successfully promoted. In the study carried out by Bennett and Cass (1988), groups made up of low ability pupils did not function very well, whereas mixed ability groups performed exceptionally well. They concluded that this may well be as a result of the lack of collaborative skills amongst the group members. The achievement of specific tasks is, of course, important. For some pupils, however, collaboration, and cooperation with others may well be a legitimate end in itself. Sociability is a desirable aim for all pupils, and one which has often been central to the philosophy of schools for pupils with learning difficulties. It is, of course, a state which cannot be reached simply through individual instruction, though that is not to deny the part which structured one-to-one teaching can play. The achievement of sociability may often be the most demanding requirement placed upon pupils and teachers alike.

When we are promoting the idea of group work, we must be clear about this issue, and should be considering the elements of an effective group, and the roles which individuals will need to play in group situations. Teachers who promote group work need to define what it is they expect the group to achieve. Negotiating and discussing this intended outcome with pupils will help to focus more clearly on the task in hand. This also applies when considering what each individual within the group is expected to contribute and gain. Pupils need to feel confidence in their own abilities to work in groups. Teachers have a vital role to play here in providing reassurance, and in helping pupils to clarify for themselves the role which they will be playing.

McCall (1983) stresses the need for some teacher direction in the organisation and working of groups. He identifies some characteristics in pupils which can lead to the failure of group work, for instance:

- authoritarianism;
- dominant cliques;
- isolationist tendencies;
- overt and hidden peer leadership.

Teachers need to become skilled in identifying which characteristics pupils have and the ways in which these will affect group composition. For example, pupils with isolationist tendencies are likely to need considerable support if they are to interact effectively in a group. Attention may need to be given to addressing their skills of communication and they may need to be placed in a group which will be supportive and sensitive to personal needs.

By contrast, pupils who are authoritarian must sometimes be checked, and placed alongside other confident pupils in order to ensure that they do not dominate the group. There may, however, be times when a dominant character will provide a useful stimulus to an otherwise ineffective group. It is important that pupils learn to play a variety of roles in group situations. If group work with pupils with severe learning difficulties is to be developed successfully, we must spend more time working on group composition. This will in turn demand that we give particular thought to group aims as well as individual needs, and that we become more efficient at managing timetables in our schools.

One final obstacle to group work is brought to our attention by Ainscow (1989). He believes that teachers have not been trained in methods of promoting group work in schools, and that there is a danger of bad practice arising as a result of insufficient understanding of the practicalities.

Where pupils are to be introduced to cooperative ways of working this has to be planned and introduced in a systematic way, as with any other new learning experience. Effectively it involves the introduction of an additional series of demands, requiring pupils to work towards objectives associated with the content of the curriculum at the same time as achieving new objectives to do with their skills in collaboration. (Ainscow, 1989, p.77)

In other words, we need to be considering the teaching of collaboration as a complex set of skills, attitudes and understanding as distinct from, but also complementary to our teaching of the task itself within a group activity. The development of self confidence and self esteem in pupils must be regarded as equally important to the acquisition of knowledge. The pupil who acquires the ability to share ideas, to collaborate with others, and to apply herself confidently in a variety of situations will attain a level of sociability which will equip her for post school life. By contrast, the pupil who has gained a set of skills and a wealth of knowledge, but whose abilities to function effectively as part of a group are limited, is likely to experience difficulties in adjusting to the many demands which a multi-faceted society will impose. The recent calls for balance in the curriculum should not be interpreted only in terms of the content, but must also consider these important issues of teaching style. This theme will be developed further in chapter five.

The word collaboration does, in fact, suggest a need for negotiation. At one level this may be between pupils, but a more fundamental issue concerns negotiation between pupils and teachers. Negotiation needs to be learned. The good negotiator is one who can give and take, who can see things from the perspective of another, and having weighed the evidence can make a decision for the common good. This may sound idealistic for many pupils with severe learning difficulties. Indeed, good negotiators are rare anywhere in society. The levels of sophistication within negotiation vary considerably, and we are not suggesting that all pupils will become effective negotiators. The beginnings of negotiation are, however, to be found in the simple making of choices, and expression of preferences. Unless teachers present opportunities for such expression, the process for many pupils will never begin.

Group work does present an opportunity for pupils to begin the early stages of negotiation, through sharing materials, helping other pupils to achieve a goal, and identifying their own strengths and weaknesses in team situations. Teachers must play a vital role in assisting pupils to see the consequences of any decision which they make, in acting as intermediaries in the negotiation process, and ensuring that all pupils have a chance to participate fully. The teacher who directs all of a pupil's activities denies a valuable opportunity for learning.

Meeting individual needs within group work

Developing approaches which will take account of individual differences whilst bringing pupils together in collaborative learning, is more challenging to teachers working with groups who have diverse needs. Well differentiated learning makes many demands upon the teacher. Not least of these is the ability to define group activities which will encompass those skills which have been identified as necessary for the development of each pupil. In order to be effective in promoting group work, the teacher needs to analyse the content of each lesson, to identify its component parts, and to match these to the needs of individual pupils and the skills, attitudes and understandings which they will need in order to become social learners. (A staff development activity addressing this can be found in NCC, 1992b). Earlier in this chapter we pointed out that not all opportunities for learning can be identified prior to the session. Hence, additional opportunities for collaboration may ensue once the session has begun.

Many problems of differentiation centre on the intentions of the curriculum. There is often a mismatch between:

Perceived curriculum and **Actual (received) curriculum**
[what the teacher   [what the pupil is learning]
believes is being
taught]

Bennett (1991, p.123) has looked at this issue in terms of what he calls the intended curriculum:

> With regard to the narrower definition of intention two trends are apparent from our studies. First, and not infrequently, the tasks that children perform are not those which the teacher intended, and second, that when tasks are observed over a long period of time there is a clear difference in the actual curriculum received by low and high attainers.

Differentiation must take account of the fact that what pupils are learning (received) is not necessarily what teachers believe they are teaching (perceived). For teachers to be successful in providing differentiated learning, however, they will need to recognise teaching as a **process** as well as a **product.**

Individuals within the group, because of their different levels of functioning, may all acquire different things from that lesson (received curriculum). Whilst all teachers need to be aware of the intended outcome of their lesson, it is equally important to have a clear idea of the learning opportunities which exist within the lesson itself. In some cases, this will mean an identification of those opportunities which exist for the teaching of specific skills. For example, a technology lesson during which pupils build a simple balance for weighing goods in a classroom shop may provide one pupil with the opportunity to develop skills in joining construction materials, whilst another is learning about simple measures, and a third concentrates upon sorting the materials to be used. At other times, the teacher may be more concerned to provide an environment to promote interaction and collaboration, possibly related to pupils solving a simple problem.

This is best illustrated through an actual lesson.

A teacher was observed working with a large group of pupils with a wide range of needs. Her lesson aimed to teach pupils that there are primary colours which, when mixed in certain combinations, produce secondary colours. Had every pupil in the group been of like ability, and had they all at the end of the lesson have learned everything that was intended about primary and secondary colours, the overall aim (**product**) would have been achieved. The range of abilities in the group was such that whilst some of the pupils grasped all of the concepts involved, many did not.

Using the original aim of the lesson as a criterion, it could be argued that the lesson failed in its stated intention because not all of the pupils achieved the aim. Careful planning should, however, include consideration of the need to provide **differentiated** learning here. Looking at the lesson as a **process,** within the group, some pupils learned that there are primary colours, red, blue and yellow, and that by mixing them in set combinations it is possible to produce orange, green and purple. Other pupils may have simply learned that by mixing some colours others are produced, and yet others may have learned that the colour which is the same as my jumper is called yellow. Each pupil learned at his or her own level.

Each pupil progressed a stage along the way to achieving the overall aim of the lesson. The skill which the teacher needs to acquire is in identifying the components of the lesson, and matching those components to the needs and skills of the pupils. Once this is successfully achieved, he will be able to plan his next lesson taking account of the level of achievement which pupils have made during the previous session. This is surely the main thrust of differentiation. Essentially, it has moved us forward from a situation in which we have attempted to plan for individuals and then tried to construct activities suitable for a class, to one in which we plan group activities whilst taking account of the needs of the individuals within it.

Developing this idea further, an awareness of pupils' individual strengths and weaknesses can help to ensure that they play a full role in collaborative learning. This relates back to the research described earlier which indicated that mixed ability groups are most successful in promoting collaborative work and facilitating learning. Amongst groups of pupils with severe learning difficulties it is quite possible to identify roles for individual pupils according to the task being undertaken.

For example, in a problem solving exercise pupils were involved in constructing a cantilever bridge to cross a space. During the process of problem solving, one pupil was selected by members of her group to sit on the end of the plank as a counterweight because she was the biggest in the group. Another pupil was selected to cross the bridge because she was the smallest in the group. Here was an example of pupils who differentiated the task for themselves based upon their practical work in solving a problem; this provided them with an understanding of what they could each contribute in this situation.

In the same activity, it was apparent that pupils assumed different roles. One pupil for instance, was quite directive, giving specific instructions to the others. Others assumed a physical role in moving planks or building parts of the bridge. One pupil even assumed the role of questioning each step of what was being done to assure himself of the logic being deployed (quality control?).

Each pupil contributed to the overall task, yet legitimately it could not be claimed at the end of the lesson that the pupils all knew the principles behind how to build a cantilever bridge. It could, however, be clearly seen that learning had taken place, and that pupils had all learned different things from the exercise. Let us also not forget the importance of the hidden curriculum. Had the pupils learned something about themselves? about their group mates? about collaboration?

Developing group work skills

Pupils in group situations will often assume a particular role. McCall (1983) has emphasised the nature of some of these roles. If learning is to be fully effective, however, it is necessary for children to learn to play several of these roles, or to adopt different roles in different situations to take account of their skills and weaknesses.

One of the difficulties of self differentiation is a tendency for pupils to gravitate to those parts of an activity in which they already feel confident. Real learning occurs when pupils tackle those parts of an activity which make new demands, and when they succeed in meeting this challenge. In order that this can occur, pupils must develop a confidence which will encourage them to see that occasional failures and mistakes are all part of the learning process. Experimentation, and investigation will inevitably result in some initial failures to achieve. Pupils must be encouraged to see that this aspect of learning relates not only to them, but is true of everyone, including those of us who are supposed to have become more sophisticated in our approach to learning. Teachers will need to address pupils' attitudes to learning by encouraging them to realise that such failures are in themselves a part of learning, and will need to encourage pupils to build upon the experiences gained. By confronting these issues, teachers can play an essential role in assisting pupils to develop a positive attitude to their own learning, and to become self confident. This will, in many instances, require a change of teacher approach and attitude. Effective group work does, however, demand a shift from the model of the teacher as instructor and source of wisdom to that of the teacher as facilitator and enabler.

Before pupils can participate effectively as members of a group, they must develop an awareness of others, and be able to see how interdependencies are established. There is an irony here, in that so much of the work which has been traditionally undertaken with pupils with learning difficulties has reinforced the dependency of pupils upon adults. Errorless learning, with its refusal to allow pupils the opportunity to learn from their mistakes, and a focus upon individual planning, has detracted from the important place which a pupil has as a member of a peer group. In many situations pupils, and particularly those with profound and multiple learning difficulties, have acquired a dependency upon specific adults, and have become largely unaware of the opportunities which exist for sharing activities with their peers. This particular group, and pupils with challenging behaviours or emotional and behavioural difficulties present the greatest demands upon the teacher intent on providing group work situations. Yet it is these pupils who probably have most to gain from working and cooperating together in groups. Such difficulties have long been acknowledged, as has the need for a systematic approach to overcoming them.

Working in pairs

An initial step towards group work must be an increased awareness of others, and a first move here can often be to develop a system of working in pairs. Even shared activities demand careful pairing to ensure compatibility of pupils. Often the teaming of a skilled pupil with one whose needs are greater and in some cases profound can have mutual benefits.

This has been no more effectively demonstrated than by the work of the late Veronica Sherborne (see for example, Sherborne, 1990) whose introduction of paired work in movement lessons enabled many pupils to place their trust in others where previously they had demonstrated apprehension and in some instances outright rejection. Sherborne's work proved effective not only with pupils with severe learning difficulties, but also in addressing the needs of pupils with emotional and behavioural difficulties, and can be seen in use in many schools for pupils with learning difficulties across the country. Equally effective in developing early relationships, and encouraging cooperation in learning was Dorothy Heathcote whose work in drama can be paralleled to that of Veronica Sherborne in movement. Heathcote recognised the importance of retaining individuality whilst encouraging cooperation and building interdependence. The pioneering work of both of these unique individuals can lay the foundations for the development of more structured group work.

It is, of course, far easier to negotiate and to share in a paired situation than it is in a larger group. Notice, for instance, the number of adults who feel more confident in speaking to one or two individuals than they do in addressing a group of people. Similarly, it is easier to share with someone who is known than with a group of relative strangers. Methods of encouraging paired work may well provide a useful stepping stone between the attention to individual planning, and the need for creating a more sociable and cooperative learning regime.

Many teachers working with pupils with severe learning difficulties have encouraged paired work. Often, however, this has been based on the tendency of pupils with similar skills and needs to gravitate naturally towards each other. The deliberate pairing of pupils with a focus upon one task is less frequently witnessed. Where it is tried, it can be effective so long as certain parameters are observed. One particular danger in the pairing of a skilled pupil with another of far greater needs is that the more skilled pupil assumes the role of minder, and does everything for their partner. Whilst this may have some social benefits, and encourages care and responsibility, it does very little to promote interactive learning. In order for such situations to be effective, more thought and planning have to be employed.

It is essential that time is given to the consideration of the tasks to be presented for paired work, and the skills of the pupils to be paired. This can be illustrated through an example taken from a classroom in a school for pupils with learning difficulties where a teacher was working with a group of 11 to 13 year old pupils following a visit to a local agricultural college. Two pupils were seated together by the teacher who talked with them about ways in which they might thank the students who had worked with them at the college. After some initial discussion, they decided to produce a picture which would record their visit, and which they could send to the students at the college in order to show them what they had seen and liked.

The pupils were asked to sort together through a box of toy farm animals, and to find a selection of animals which they had seen at the college. The pupils did this together, eliminating some animals which they had not seen at the college farm, but retaining a selection of farm animals which they set out on the table before them. The teacher then suggested that one of the pupils should draw a picture which included all of the selected animals, whilst the other should write the names of the animals on sticky labels to put on the picture. The pupils set about their tasks, and after fifteen minutes had completed this part of the activity. The pupils now had a selection of labels with the names of various animals, cow, sheep and so on, and a colourful picture which represented the animals at the college.

This picture may well have been fairly clear to the pupil who drew it, but for most observers it would have been difficult to distinguish the individual animals. The teacher therefore suggested that the two pupils should discuss where they should stick the labels to show each of the individual animals. This involved the one pupil reading the labels to the other (who could not read) who then indicated where the various animals in the picture were located. When the teacher returned to them, the labels were in place, and between them the pupils were able to explain their work.

This example of paired work took account of the individual needs of both pupils, and provided an opportunity for them to practise their particular skills in writing and drawing. It also encouraged them to share in the production of one piece of work, and to discuss and negotiate both the methods to be used and the final outcome. Such an approach with the teacher acting as facilitator can be replicated in many other teaching situations.

The move from paired work to group work will inevitably take time, and it is essential that pupils learn to work with several other individuals before venturing into structured group work. Given the right opportunities, many pupils do understand that they have personal skills and strengths which allow them to play particular roles in groups. An important role for the teacher is to build upon these strengths in group work situations before pupils are encouraged to adopt other roles which do not necessarily come so easily to them. Once the move from paired work to group work is to be made, it is obviously best to ensure that those members of a group with whom pupils are expected to work are known to them, and have been involved in paired work with them.

Jigsawing

As with all effective teaching, an essential part of developing group work must be the planning stage. An emphasis on group work should not mean that the needs of the individual are forgotten. Indeed the converse should be true. Various methods of ensuring full pupil involvement in group work have been developed. The choice of which method to use will often depend upon the intended outcomes of the lesson, and the needs of individual pupils.

One approach which has been used successfully with pupils with severe learning difficulties (Rose, 1991) is called 'jigsawing'. In this method, which was largely developed through the work of Johnson et al (Johnson and Johnson, 1987; Johnson et al, 1990), an activity is broken down into tasks which are interdependent, and which are defined according to the needs and abilities of individual pupils. In its simplest form this approach can be illustrated as in figures 5 and 6.

Each piece of the jigsaw is dependent upon the others and there is thus a need for regular communication between individuals and groups throughout each session of learning based upon this model. The teacher has an opportunity to develop compatible groups which will encourage the development of skills, learning attitudes and understanding, and can also address individual needs in a group work context.

Jigsawing is without doubt an effective way of providing group work for pupils, including those with profound and multiple learning difficulties. It is, however, more useful in some situations than in others. Certainly it is best deployed in practical activities such as art and craft, technology, cookery and science where it can ensure full participation of pupils, encourages interaction, and takes account of individual needs. It does make considerable demands upon teacher organisation and classroom management, and may not lend itself well to teaching the more traditional parts of the curriculum.

Other methods of group work have, of course, been tried with pupils with learning difficulties. Envoying, in which several groups operate within a project, from time to time each group sending 'envoys' to report to the others on progress, and provide information vital to the success of the project is one which has also proved effective. A simple example of this was seen in a school for pupils with learning difficulties in which pupils had visited a cardboard box manufacturer. On return to school, one group was established to make some sweets during a cookery lesson, whilst another group were asked to design and make containers in technology. Having decided on the type of sweets, their size, shape and consistency, the first group sent two pupils to provide this information to the second group making boxes. On completion of the boxes, two pupils were sent to the first group to try their boxes out, and to receive comments from the sweet makers. On the basis of this evaluation, and having seen the sweets, the box makers reported back to their group, made alterations, and completed their design. This type of approach encourages cooperation between pupils from two groups, and makes demands upon skills of communication, evaluation and negotiation.

Define the task and
intended outcomes
with the whole group.

Give each pupil or
group of pupils
different parts of
the material.

Give each pupil or
group of pupils the
information needed
to complete their
part of the task.

Give each pupil or
group of pupils a
distinct but vital
role to play in
completing their part
of the task.

Encourage self differentiation.

Bring the whole group
back together to
evaluate the outcomes
of the task.

Figure 5: Jigsawing

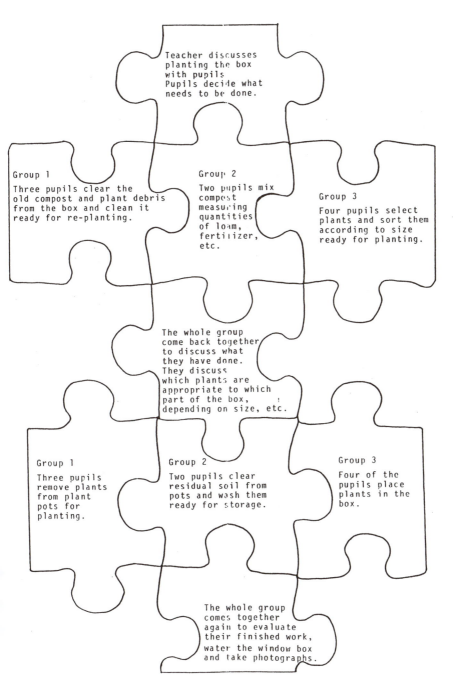

Teacher discusses planting the box with pupils
Pupils decide what needs to be done.

Group 1
Three pupils clear the old compost and plant debris from the box and clean it ready for re-planting.

Group 2
Two pupils mix compost measuring quantities of loam, fertilizer, etc.

Group 3
Four pupils select plants and sort them according to size ready for planting.

The whole group come back together to discuss what they have done. They discuss which plants are appropriate to which part of the box, depending on size, etc.

Group 1
Three pupils remove plants from plant pots for planting.

Group 2
Two pupils clear residual soil from pots and wash them ready for storage.

Group 3
Four of the pupils place plants in the box.

The whole group comes together again to evaluate their finished work, water the window box and take photographs.

Figure 6: Example of a jigsawed activity: preparing a window box for school

Conclusion

This chapter has been concerned with examining issues of teaching styles which give a greater involvement and responsibility to pupils. Group work is seen as vital to the achievement of this. For many pupils currently in schools for pupils with learning difficulties, and indeed for some in mainstream schools, these ideals may appear to be somewhat distant. The approaches used with pupils with severe learning difficulties to date have often centred upon control, instruction and skill based training. This chapter has advocated greater pupil autonomy, and a move towards enabling pupils to become more effective in assisting with their own learning. It would be optimistic to suggest that such a transition can be easily achieved, but it is to be hoped that some of the ideas currently being deployed by teachers in schools may move us a little nearer to this overall goal. Much will depend upon teachers being prepared to adapt their teaching styles to an approach which encourages pupils to share in the responsibility for managing their own learning.

Chapter Four

Management of the Curriculum

Introduction

Currently, there is a perceived need for schools to demonstrate that they are 'curriculum driven' if they wish to be seen as keeping abreast of the latest developments, changes and legislation in education. This represents a major shift in thinking which has occurred recently partly in response to the National Curriculum.

Until recently, 'progressive' schools proclaimed a rhetoric concerned with being 'needs driven'. Staff claimed that pupils were individuals with a broad range of differing individual needs, which could best be served by creating individual curriculum packages. This model developed in response to the 1981 Education Act and the machinery of statementing and annual review which was intended as a means of ensuring each pupil's entitlement to a relevant, tailor-made, individually-fitted curriculum.

The plethora of change with which schools have been confronted in recent years, and the effects which such radical changes inevitably produce, will necessitate a shift in the way in which the curriculum is managed and delivered. Too many issues have arrived in schools at once. Those concerned to provide a first-rate service to pupils with learning difficulties are wrestling with the changes which have been thrust upon them.

This chapter describes some of the ways in which schools may effectively manage changes in the curriculum. The curriculum itself is inevitably influenced by, and dependent upon a whole range of other issues, the interdependency of which will be examined here. School staff need to be aware of the systems and processes which will help them to come to terms with the current, at times stormy, educational climate. The successful schools of the near future will be those most able to adapt, but especially those most willing to take full advantage of recent legislation for the ultimate benefit of the pupils for whom they have responsibilities.

School development planning

Ensuring that all staff are aware of the school's aims and are fully involved in a regular process of review is a major step in the effective management of the school curriculum. Schools have a responsibility to produce development plans, and to identify areas of the curriculum, and its management which should be prioritised for progress and improvement over a given period of time. The process through which this is done is described more fully in the advice that was issued to schools in 1990 (DES, 1989c). For many schools, the production and management of a development plan presents a new challenge. Sadly, the level of training and support which has been provided to undertake this process has been variable (West and Ainscow, 1991).

The curriculum will have a high profile in most school planning processes but will not constitute the whole plan. Yet even those areas of the development plan which centre upon other aspects of school management, such as finance or staff development will inevitably have to reflect the curricular priorities. The National Curriculum has made demands upon schools which reach far beyond interpretation and implementation. Amongst these have been a redirection of the in-service education of teachers, the redistribution of financial support to provide for what may previously have been minority or even untapped subjects, and a reappraisal of job descriptions with teachers assuming responsibilities for redefined curricular areas. All of these changes are a consequence of the Education Reform Act and other recent legislation. This legislation has brought about unparalleled demands upon school staff who have been expected to take up the challenge of the National Curriculum whilst dealing with the local management of schools, a re-emphasis upon appraisal, further delegation of in-service education responsibilities, and a changing relationship with governors.

Curriculum development

Management of the school curriculum is an ongoing challenge. The effective curriculum is one which is perpetually under review, modified to meet the changing nature and demands of the society in which we live. For this reason, no curriculum document will ever be conclusive, but will rather reflect a given situation at a particular time. Documents should, however, indicate the philosophy of a school. They should provide not only clear guidance for staff on matters of curriculum content, delivery, recording and assessment, but should assist in the provision of a school ethos which is tailored to meet a specific population.

Changes have occurred in the ways in which special educational needs are addressed, with a greater emphasis upon integration. These have been paralleled by changes in obstetric and paediatric practices which have resulted in a greater number of pupils with profound and multiple learning difficulties entering schools. Similarly, changes in medical management have increased life expectancy for some pupils, altering the population throughout the school. This has required a reappraisal of teaching approaches, curriculum content and classroom management. Such a reappraisal was clearly necessary in many schools even prior to the arrival of the National Curriculum. However, the National Curriculum has been an accelerator, if not a catalyst in this process.

Ownership of the curriculum is a key factor if a school is to be effective in educating its pupils. Recent legislation has reiterated responsibilities within the curriculum and demands that a partnership be established between all bodies responsible for providing an education to pupils. The roles to be played by teachers, therapists, governors, and to some extent parents in the development of the curriculum have come under close scrutiny. The responsibilities of Local Education Authorities, previously quite well defined, are becoming less clear and are in danger of erosion.

There is a danger that the current pressures on schools could lead to a dilution of sound curriculum development principles. A whole school approach to curriculum development should provide opportunities for the entire school community to discuss its principles and intentions. The headteacher, staff and governors will each have their own perception of the school and its pupils, their needs and priorities. More general discussion of curriculum policy can ensure that all agencies have increased awareness of the purposes and needs of the school; and this can prevent possible conflicts of interest as the school progresses. Pressures of time and the weight of demands made upon schools could lead to an unhealthy cutting of corners. The practical nature of curriculum development needs careful consideration before schools embark upon any campaign to effect change.

There is no doubt that the quickest way to produce curriculum documentation, guidance for teachers and systems of delivery, is for one individual to sit down and undertake the work. This person, sometimes the headteacher, more often the deputy head or a curriculum coordinator becomes familiar with new documentation and legislation, interprets it for colleagues and hands it on to staff for implementation. Undoubtedly, this provides a learning process for the individual. It is also a method which may be regarded by colleagues with some relief at a time when we are all inundated with change and too much to do. This mirrors the method by which much of the Education Reform Act was put into place, with information supplied at such a rate that teachers and others in education had little time to react and provide a considered response. Such a technique may have been effective for getting legislation quickly into place, but as a method of curriculum management it is sterile, and probably does no more than postpone some of the issues which need to be confronted.

Curriculum development needs time, a commodity in short supply in schools. A first principle must be that we refuse to hurry curriculum into place at the expense of quality education. Certainly schools need to review their curricular approaches and content, and to examine current practice in relation to changes in legislation. This must be done in a thoughtful way which will promote good practice and ensure a better quality of education for pupils.

Responsibility for the curriculum

Beginning with the establishment of a set of principles can be a painful process for a school, but will save time as curriculum development gathers momentum. In any curriculum document the principles, whilst of paramount importance, are likely to be contained on a few sides of paper, whereas the schemes of work and elaboration of content will inevitably provide the bulk of the document. Schools need to discuss central issues such as pupil involvement, reporting to parents, self advocacy, recording and assessment, group work and differentiation and relationships with other professionals, which will determine the way in which the curriculum is eventually delivered. The development of policy in these areas should then be reflected throughout not only the curriculum documents, but also the way in which pupils are taught.

The role of governors

This process provides schools with an opportunity to fully involve governors and parents. The notion that governors should assume responsibility for the curriculum is often seen as idealistic. The current practice in many schools, and even in some where bold attempts have been made to involve governors, is still to pay a token regard to the responsibilities which governors must be prepared to assume when they take office. Adequate training and guidance must be provided and encouragement given to governors to spend time in classrooms, in order to grasp the realities and fulfil their tasks proficiently.

Legislation has made it clear that governors' powers are far reaching, but with power comes responsibility. Their role in the management of the school will include an involvement in the school curriculum. Schools must be realistic. Not all governors will become actively involved in curriculum development or delivery, some will focus their attention upon other aspects of the school's work. Matters of school policy and principle are the responsibility of governors who should be encouraged to discuss issues such as those outlined above.

Many schools now have a sub-committee of the governing body which addresses curriculum issues. Through these sub-committees a few governors become more fully involved in curriculum matters and share ideas with staff and parents. This is a more realistic way of enabling at least some governors to keep themselves informed on curriculum matters, and to make a contribution to discussions. These governors may then report back to governors' meetings and play a full part in curriculum discussions. At a time when local management of schools has seen the development of governors' finance committees and building maintenance committees, it is unreasonable to expect every governor to play a major part in curriculum development. In practice, much curricular responsibility will remain delegated to the headteacher.

The role of parents

If consultation and planning with governors is important, then the involvement of parents is no less so. Many parents have been confused by the plethora of information which has emerged from the DFE, National Curriculum Council and Schools Assessment and Examination Council in recent years. In order to assist them to develop informed opinions, schools must take responsibility for the dissemination of information. Parent governors may well have a vital role here. As schools work on curriculum development they must endeavour to consult parents and keep them informed. Parents often provide valuable insights into the management and development of their sons and daughters which can assist with devising methods of curricular delivery.

At a time of rapid change in education, there will inevitably be issues which parents will need to discuss with professionals. For example, the notions of pupil decision making and empowerment are likely to be controversial. The implementation of these objectives within a school may lead to conflict unless parents are fully consulted and involved in the planning process.

Management of recording and reporting

The establishment of principles on recording and reporting may be a long and involved process. All staff need to be fully involved, and to have opportunities to contribute their opinions. It is essential that all staff have access to relevant documentation and to examples of practice from elsewhere. Some issues will reflect ongoing reviews of recording while others will have resulted from recent legislation and guidance.

We may take, for example, the involvement of pupils in recording their own progress, and in the development of records of achievement. This has been the focus of attention for some time in a number of schools, but for others has not yet surfaced as an issue. In both mainstream and schools for pupils with learning difficulties, students are rarely given ownership of the record of achievement. Sometimes the record of achievement is written exclusively by the teacher in the presence of the student, or discussed with them once completed. In other cases, the students' comments are censored or edited because of perceived criticism of the teacher or the school.

For many schools, involvement of pupils would be a brave step. Before staff can embark upon an effective discussion of this matter, they require access to examples, and to hear from teachers who have been involved in the use of pupil recording techniques. Opportunities to visit schools which have established practice may prove helpful, particularly where teachers are provided with a brief to gain specific information. In many schools innovations such as pupil self recording may be in evidence in some classrooms but with no overall cohesion or policy.

The issue of recording and assessment is fraught with difficulties which have troubled schools over many years. Examples of good practice and principles abound (see in particular, Lawson, 1992) yet this still appears to be an area with many pitfalls and confusions. A whole school policy on recording and assessment is essential. Not only does this promote continuity as pupils move from class to class, but it also assists with planning, identifying individual and group needs and reporting to parents. The role of school records coordinator should be allocated to one member of staff who will prepare records of achievement and collect and analyse the evidence for the evaluation of teaching and materials.

Effective recording systems are ones which are easily used, are not over time consuming, ignore superfluous information, and are readily understood by everyone. They need to demonstrate where pupils are now in their learning, and to indicate the direction in which they are to proceed. Simple recording systems which collect essential information do not preclude staff keeping their own records in whatever format, and with whatever detail they see as helpful to themselves. Involvement of parents and other professionals in the devising of a recording system will certainly assist in defining the information which is essential. In particular, parents can often put into the most concise terms what it is they wish to know about their son or daughter's progress.

All schools are required to report annually to parents which has led to a reconsideration of the ways in which this can be streamlined with other demands. Effective planning will enable links to be made and overlaps to be avoided between recording, records of achievement and the annual review procedures. Pupil attendance at annual reviews often serves to sharpen an awareness in professionals of the language which they use and the clarity of reports. An absence of jargon serves not only parents and pupils well, but comes as a great relief to the majority of teachers and therapists.

Schools should not forget the pupil in this process. Often pupils have very definite ideas about the things which they would like to see recorded, and in some instances these may differ from those which we, as professionals, or their parents have considered important. The collection of evidence using photographs or pupils' work is one way in which pupils can be involved in decision making. Pupils may have particular reasons for choosing a piece of work which they want to be included or excluded which conflicts with the teacher's views and their opinions need to be considered. Chapter five will consider the part which pupils can play in the management of their own learning.

Establishing whole school policy

School staff should beware the temptation to do something because everyone else is doing it. Whether it be pupil self recording, the development of a modular curriculum, or any other central issue, schools must find their own salvation. The individuality of schools, particularly at a time of greater centralisation, is of great importance. School staff who establish principles and adopt practices of which they have ownership are likely to be more effective.

Having advocated a whole school approach to matters of curriculum development, one also has to accept that individuals have differing skills and abilities and will therefore make a variety of contributions. Since the introduction of the National Curriculum, many schools have found the need to re-examine the provision of in-service education in order to increase expertise in subjects which they have previously given little consideration. A generic approach to teaching has been the norm for pupils with learning difficulties, with subject specialists being scarce. Where such specialists have existed they have often been in areas such as physical education, art, craft and music.

The National Curriculum has highlighted the value of subjects such as science, geography and technology for pupils with learning difficulties. Teachers have set out to examine ways of delivering these to pupils with a diverse range of needs. During our work with colleagues in the National Curriculum Development Team (severe learning difficulties) based at the Cambridge Institute of Education we saw many examples of teachers addressing these specific curricular areas with pupils with learning difficulties (NCC, 1992a).

There is no doubt that teachers of pupils with learning difficulties need considerable help and training to deliver subjects in which they may have little or no expertise. This will influence the speed with which curricular change can be effected. Schools need to ensure that staff who are expected to deliver curricular areas have received adequate training to do so. Similarly, institutions of higher education and whatever local training agencies may exist in the future are required to increase their awareness of this and work with schools to provide training and support, as is current practice in relation to some subject areas. Similarly, the format of future initial training of teachers must reflect the changing needs of schools and those with responsibility for this training must be prepared to share expertise with school staff.

Resource management

Many schools who have developed the role of curriculum coordinator now find a need to redefine this in light of National Curriculum demands. The role of the coordinator has become one of resources and staff development manager. Schools have realised the need to develop resources in areas such as science and technology which may in the past have been limited. The organisation of resources and matching of resources to curriculum modules has become a time consuming task.

Schools which have referenced their curriculum to the programmes of study have found great value in developing curricular packages and in producing resource packs to accompany these. Whilst this is initially time consuming, it does ultimately save on teacher preparation time and overcomes some of the frustrations associated with finding the right materials for each lesson. This requires someone who is sufficiently organised to ensure that resource packages are updated, staff informed of contents and their application and consumables replaced. It also places an onus on staff to ensure that the coordinator is informed about materials which need replacing or repair, with suggestions for new materials and the development of new teaching plans or modules. The National Curriculum with its emphasis upon key stages, attainment targets and programmes of study lends itself well to the development of school resource banks.

The development of resources is expensive. This can provide major difficulties for the small school with limited finances. More schools are realising the value of sharing resources and coordinating their use. This is particularly evidenced in those schools which have pursued a cross-curricular approach. By planning together in small cluster groups, staff have enabled resource banks to be passed from one school to another and thus to benefit a greater number of pupils and teachers. This approach has been used by some primary schools over a considerable period of time.

Where individual subjects are taught the subject coordinator can build a resource bank in one area of the school and monitor its use. Cross-curricular approaches require the integration of materials from more than one subject area related to specific lessons or groups of lessons. Thought needs to be given to the situation and accessibility of materials, issues of age appropriateness and safety. For example, the level of reading content in worksheets will inevitably need to be matched to the needs of individual pupils, and similarly, tools which may be safely used by some children would be wholly inappropriate for others.

Staff development

In addition to the development of resources, the provision of effective staff development has become a focus for school coordinators. The delegation of in-service education budgets to schools and the use of regular training days has resulted in different approaches to in-service education in various parts of the country. Staff working with pupils with learning difficulties often felt that the in-service education programme provided by local authorities failed to meet their needs and have been able to tailor their own packages. The school development plan can assist with ensuring that staff development matches curriculum development and staff's own personal and professional needs.

With increasing pressure upon school budgets, it will be essential that the budget holders are fully involved in discussion with staff to ensure that such a match is made. This will inevitably mean that in-service education will need to be closely focused and driven by school needs. This emphasis upon schools identifying their own in service requirements must, however, be preferable to opting into a programme which is externally driven, so long as there is an awareness of the potential danger of becoming isolated, and of encouraging insular attitudes.

Just as schools need to share resources, so must they become proficient in meeting their in-service education needs through collaboration with others. The use of 'cluster' days, where local schools combine for training, or county wide option days for schools with similarly identified needs can prove helpful. Not only do these make economic sense, with schools pooling financial resources to bring in a speaker, or hire facilities, but also they provide an opportunity for staff to share experiences and learn from each other.

Some local authorities have encouraged networks, or support groups for coordinators of specific subjects. Here teachers can meet together to develop materials, exchange ideas, and plan future joint ventures. There are several examples of outstanding curricular materials for pupils with learning difficulties being developed by such groups (East Sussex County Council, 1990; Humberside County Council, 1990; 1992).

Staff roles and responsibilities

If a teacher is to assume responsibility for the coordination of resources or staff development or both, it would be unreasonable to expect such a person also to coordinate all other aspects of curriculum development. The need for subject coordinators has been acknowledged by many primary schools and schools for pupils with learning difficulties and has actually been required by some LEAs. This may present problems for these schools for two reasons.

First, many of these schools are small, and by their nature have only a few teachers which will inevitably mean some teachers accepting responsibility for more than one curricular area. Secondly, the number of specialist teachers for some subjects in primary schools and schools for pupils with learning difficulties is very limited, which can cause an understandable reluctance on the part of staff to assume responsibility for an area in which they feel they lack expertise. In order to minimise the anxieties which these two problems can cause, schools need to develop strategies and systems which will anticipate difficulties. One such move may be to appoint a subject coordinator well in advance of the time when that subject is to become 'high profile'. For example, in anticipation that in four terms time technology will be an area of particular concern, a coordinator could be appointed with time to receive in-service education, to visit places of expertise, to talk with members of the inspectorate, and generally to improve knowledge and understanding of the subject. Participation in county wide or local technology groups, where they exist, may help to develop a network of support.

The National Curriculum subjects have been taught in mainstream secondary schools for a long time, and there is a wealth of experience and expertise to be shared with colleagues. Planning ahead will enable schools to predict budgetary requirements, and to anticipate times when resourcing needs for a particular subject may be high. Subject coordinators should not be left to work in isolation. Headteachers will need to provide an adequate level of support for the coordinator to complete his tasks. This may involve the allocation of supply cover from the school in-service education budget. It may also require the head to play a liaison role between the subject inspector and the coordinator, and to ensure that the coordinator receives all relevant information coming into school.

Schools which intend to address a specific curricular area might begin with one in which they feel relatively comfortable. Assuming that the school has already established a set of principles as discussed above, they may then nominate a subject coordinator. The role of this person should be carefully defined. Job descriptions often define responsibilities, they seldom refer to rights and needs. It has oft been a cry within education that teachers have not been given adequate resources to 'do the job'. Schools must therefore ensure that if subject coordinators are appointed, they are given the support which they need.

The first need is for the full support of the school management. In a small school which has very few senior posts, a subject coordinator will feel that they are well down the line of the school hierarchy. This person will be required to lead curriculum sessions which are attended by more senior members of the staff. In these circumstances, the subject coordinator must be given the confidence to make decisions and to take a lead, knowing that they do so with the full backing of the head and the governors.

The subject coordinator needs to know from the outset what resources are available to him. Frustrations soon mount when a coordinator makes plans only to find that they are thwarted through lack of resources. The whole staff should produce a time plan for meetings, the production of materials, visits, staff development and other requirements. The head-teacher will need to advise on dates which will affect this schedule, such as meetings of the school governors' curriculum sub-committee, or other matters which will need to be dealt with by staff. The subject coordinator must be given some freedom to direct these issues.

Teachers put into this role will give a considerable amount of their own time to the development of the school. With these roles come many pressures, and staff need to be aware of these and to avoid adding to them by imposing restrictive time plans. Subject coordinators must ensure that they keep all staff informed and wherever possible, fully involved. Consideration must be given to the roles which assistants and other professionals play in the school and the expertise they have to offer. They need to be aware of specific teacher and class needs, take account of a variety of teaching styles and strengths and weaknesses in staff understanding of the subject.

Other members of staff need to be clear about their roles. It is unhelpful for staff to sit back and assume that because someone has a responsibility to coordinate a curricular area, they themselves have no further duties in that area. The reality in most schools is that teachers will teach most subjects either in a discrete way, or as part of an overall curriculum package. It is therefore essential that all staff play some role in supporting the subject coordinator. Above all, staff must be prepared to share and discuss ideas, to express opinions and to provide examples from their own experience and practice. This sharing will enable them to take ownership and responsibility for any curricular materials produced.

Headteachers have particular responsibilities for the curriculum. Their first must surely be as good practitioners in the classroom, leading by example, and showing a willingness to deploy new and sometimes difficult changes themselves. They should ensure that credit is given to staff for their work by bringing it to the attention of governors, parents, inspectors and officers. If staff are to be expected to give of their time and expertise to interpret documents, and to find ways of applying them in schools, they are deserving of some recognition of their work. In the past many schools have been reluctant to share their ideas. This is particularly sad in schools for pupils with learning difficulties whose staff are attempting to confront the same issues across the country. By publicising their work, schools should not be interpreted as saying 'we have found the answer', but rather seen to be demonstrating a particular way of addressing an issue related to their own situation. Much of the most helpful material to have been circulated since the introduction of the National Curriculum has come directly from schools or groups of schools.

Some schools and local authorities have combined with universities and other higher education establishments to provide teachers with accreditation for their work. Headteachers have an opportunity here to support their staff in a way that will ensure that they receive recognition which can be beneficial to both individual and institutional development.

Curricular audit

The need for careful evaluation of teaching has been apparent and well documented over many years, (Eisner, 1985; Holly and Southworth, 1989; Hopkins, 1985; Reid et al, 1987). The application of evaluative techniques, other than simplistic checklists or erroneous psychometric measures, in the education of pupils with learning difficulties has been less frequently reported (Batty et al, 1987; Moon and Oliver, 1985; Newman and Rose, 1990). The National Curriculum has emphasised the need for a more detailed examination of all aspects of curricular delivery, content, and construction in all schools.

Consider the old joke about the lost traveller seeking directions from an elderly fellow sitting reflectively at a country crossroads. The rural sage scratches his head and says: 'Well, if I were you I wouldn't start from here'. Such can sometimes be the nature of curricular audit.

For school staff, like the lost traveller, 'here' is the starting place, like it or not. Inspectors and advisers are sometimes just as helpful as the rural sage. They may also wish to identify a better starting place. Forced to depend upon inner resources, lost souls can do worse than attempting to identify their position in an unfamiliar landscape.

An early task of the subject coordinator, supported by colleagues, is to conduct some form of curricular audit. The importance of this stage in curriculum development was highlighted in *Curriculum Guidance 3* (NCC, 1990a). Procedures for auditing in schools for pupils with learning difficulties were further discussed in *Curriculum Guidance 9* (NCC, 1992a).

- review existing curricular content;
- match existing provision to stated curricular needs and principles, and to the needs of the National Curriculum;
- help in the formulation of the school development plan;
- give reassurance to staff about existing good practice;
- identify needs for development and resourcing.

Auditing is a process whereby staff can:

Several approaches to auditing exist. Most involve teachers recording the activities of a pupil or group of pupils over a predefined period of time. This can be achieved either through observation by a non-participating member of staff, which may be difficult to arrange in some schools, or through careful recording of activities by the teacher. Where teaching is cross-curricular or of a non subject-specific type, the teacher may wish to note all of those aspects of a lesson or series of lessons which can be referenced to a specific curricular area. For example, in a drama lesson the teacher may note all those aspects which could be related to English and music. In subject based teaching, the teacher may wish to be more specific and to note, for example, which areas of English and music from the National Curriculum are being covered.

Many schools have conducted audits of timetables. This is because of the general assumption that timetables represent a picture of experiences offered to pupils. An analytic glance over a few timetables suggests that this is not the case. Many timetables in schools for pupils with learning difficulties, in particular, contain a range of seemingly strange items indicating that 1:1 or 'individual activities' occupy whole mornings. In some mainstream as well as schools for pupils with learning difficulties notions of 'topic', or 'options' will occur, usually in the afternoon slots. These headings describe teaching styles rather than subjects or curricular content. It may indeed be valid to conduct an audit of teaching styles, but it is questionable whether this is the best way to do it.

Similarly, timetables can be found with headings such as 'soft play' or 'minibus'. These are examples of logistical signposts, reminding staff of when they have access to certain resources. It may be sensible to conduct an audit of resources and how they are allocated and used, but again this may not be the best way to do it.

Other spaces on timetables will be occupied by genuine activity headings, for example, 'play', 'story', or 'swimming'. Rather more problematically there may be headings like 'basic skills' or more contemporary but equally obscure 'P.S.E.' (personal and social education). These headings may again be useful indicators for the teacher, but they do not reveal which basic skills or which aspects of P.S.E. will be addressed during the identified sessions. Some schools have now changed their timetable headings in line with the National Curriculum, and the fortunate timetable auditor may find greater subject clarity represented by titles for sessions such as 'English', 'maths', or 'technology'. The subtle seeker after truth will, however, wish to peek behind even these timetable titles, for they may hide a rich stew of complexities.

Lessons in schools are never entirely subject specific, even when they may have a specific subject focus. The headings on a timetable may provide a very broad idea of the shape of the pupils' day, but they will be liable to tell the observer as much, or more, about where pupils are located in the school, or about how they are being taught, as they will about what they are learning. For example, a teacher uses the swimming session as a means of providing sensory stimulation. In curricular audit terms, the swimming session may therefore provide pupils with a set of experiences linked closely to the scientific notion of first hand investigation of events. In a similar way, sessions on the technology-focused integrated schemes of work this particular half term, will offer opportunities for pupils to develop their communication skills as they are encouraged to express preferences, negotiate roles in a team, and later, express their opinions regarding the artefacts which they have created.

The main point of this argument, is that a timetable audit may indicate little of any value about the actual learning opportunities offered to pupils.

Techniques of pupil shadowing and teacher auditing described in detail elsewhere (NCC, 1992a; NCC, 1992b; Sebba and Fergusson, 1991; Sebba et al, 1991) will prove more revealing in these terms. This will especially apply where auditors select categories with due regard to the purposes of their enquiry.

For instance, it will be possible to conduct an audit in terms of National Curriculum headings such as 'speaking and listening', 'handling data', or 'forces and their effects'. It will also be possible to conduct a different audit of the same sessions under headings such as 'problem solving', 'using information technology', or 'fine motor' in order to analyse opportunities to practise cross-curricular skills. Again, the same sessions may be audited for learning styles, by employing such headings as 'interaction with peers', 'collaborating in group activity', or 'attending to solitary task'.

All of these audits may be instructive and they represent only a few of the possibilities. They will offer ways of discovering what pupils are experiencing, practising and learning in terms of curricular content: how pupils are being taught, how they are learning in terms of particular styles: and whether resources and environments are being used to their best advantage. The well conducted audit should give the teacher a picture of current curricular content as provided by specific teachers or received by individual pupils. It should also indicate any obvious areas where coverage is lacking when matched either to the National Curriculum, or to required curricular content as defined by the school.

Application

Whilst the development of the school curriculum is likely to be facilitated through a whole school approach, the realities of timetabling and school organisation are likely to become the responsibility of one or two individuals. An early reaction to the National Curriculum was to claim that the timetable was already under strain, and therefore the inclusion of subjects such as geography, technology and history was likely to have the effect of watering down the existing school curriculum. This, of course, assumed that these were to be taught as discrete subjects, which in most primary schools and schools for pupils with learning difficulties would in fact have been a move away from the norm of school organisation. By far the majority of these schools teach integrated subjects, recognising for instance, the mathematics and scientific content in cookery lessons, or means of developing an understanding of language in physical education.

Earlier in this chapter we discussed the role of the subject coordinators. In the development of integrated schemes of work these people will have a definite role to play in matching content to their given subjects, ensuring breadth and balance of subject coverage, developing teacher skills and collating resources. Although they may not always be directly involved in curricular delivery, they need to assist with the design and implementation of the one off lessons concerned with developing skills. An example of an occasion when such intervention may be seen as helpful would be in the case of a specialist science teacher addressing the skills involved in using scientific apparatus prior to the woodland lesson described in the previous chapter. This may take the form of both direct teaching of pupils and staff training. In the example given, it may well be that some staff have never used a pooter, or even know what one is. In such circumstances the subject coordinator would assume a training and advisory role.

A cross-curricular approach needs to take account not only of curricular content, but also of individual needs as was discussed in chapter three. Teachers need skills that will enable them to manage group situations, to differentiate in order to meet individual needs, and to record effectively. Here, the subject coordinator needs to be in constant discussion with class teachers in order to provide ideas and to ensure the ordering of materials which are suitable for the pupils to be taught.

Team planning

In the school for pupils with learning difficulties of all ages, there are several logistical constraints which are likely to cause difficulties including the management and distribution of resources. These problems often start with the buildings themselves, where a school may have, for example, a craft room or cookery room with work surfaces too high to provide access for younger pupils. Similarly, the headteacher or other staff with responsibility for the ordering of resources in an all age school will inevitably find himself ordering expensive equipment which is suitable for use with only a small proportion of the school's population. This often results in the school budget being overstretched and compromise over the equipment provided within the school.

The demands made upon limited resources where every pupil in the school is focused upon one area of study can present major problems. Such difficulties can be compounded by the whole school adopting the same integrated scheme of work and many all age schools have found it easier to operate several schemes at once with different age groups tackling different schemes. Here too some consideration needs to be given to the role which subject coordinators play. Some coordinators have found difficulties in dealing with the broad age spread of all age schools. It is easier for the coordinator to build a team which is representative of the whole school. This team, or curricular area group will usually consist of staff (not necessarily teachers) from each section of the school who will represent the needs and ideas of that section. Here, the subject expertise of the coordinator is likely to be brought into focus, assisting the staff from each section of the school to interpret the subject in relation to their own pupils.

Effective use of cross-curricular approaches requires good long term planning. A common concern in schools for pupils with learning difficulties centres upon the over repetition of activities. There is no doubt that repetition in itself can be a useful means of reinforcing learning. This is particularly true of skills based activities which follow a set pattern, such as laying a table, or dressing. Behavioural approaches made particular use of repetition with a high degree of success for teaching discrete skills.

In more generalised teaching, however, repetition can be a source of teacher and pupil frustration. How often in a staffroom have we overheard conversations which follow the pattern of 'Oh, are you doing farms with your group? I remember when Mr Smith did farms with them two years ago.' The repetition of work on farms itself is not necessarily a bad thing. It is essential that the content of the integrated scheme of work will build upon the work carried out two years ago and move pupils on in their experiences and knowledge; new activities will be introduced and new skills developed. It is equally important that pupils will have the opportunity to recall work previously undertaken and apply this in the new, integrated scheme of work on farms.

Many schools have found that the National Curriculum has assisted them in forward planning of integrated schemes of work through use of the programmes of study. Planning from the programmes of study rather than the attainment targets ensures breadth of curricular coverage. This will also assist with recognising the overlap between subjects and recording. Some schools have planned integrated schemes of work several years in advance, and have defined these areas according to the curricular coverage required. Such a process requires staff to gain a detailed knowledge of curricular documents and to work collaboratively to ensure that pupils follow a logical progression through their school lives. In many schools for pupils with severe learning difficulties, it is likely that pupils will be working within levels 1 to 3 of the National Curriculum for an extended period. This can be helpful for staff who wish to make use of repetition and reinforcement as a means of supporting learning.

If long term plans are to be developed within a school which will project the passage of pupils through the curriculum for the whole of their school lives, it is essential that this planning is conducted on a whole school basis. Even where planning is conducted on a lower school/upper school basis it is necessary for staff from these two departments to meet together regularly in order to ensure continuity.

The extended team

Earlier in the chapter we discussed the role which governors and parents may play in the process of curriculum development. Some schools have been making full use of parents in curricular delivery for some time. Involvement of parents in the development process assists with the delivery as it can ensure that parents as well as professionals have a clearer understanding of intended outcomes.

Similarly, the valuable role which can be played by therapists is an area which needs to be expanded beyond the intervention model. Particularly in a cross-curricular approach, speech therapists, occupational therapists or physiotherapists need to see how their own aims for pupils can be incorporated into the teaching situation. Many of the exercises planned by therapists can be put into the context of a lesson in group situations as was described in chapter three. This promotes socialisation and interaction, and overcomes the frustration felt by many teachers who see their pupils being withdrawn from lessons for extended periods, which interferes with usual timetable arrangements.

Involvement of other professionals does, of course, have major implications for information sharing and communication. If we expect therapists to work as part of a team then we must also expect to involve them in staff development discussions, and in the whole process of development and delivery. There is still a potential conflict in many schools between the priorities of therapists and those of teachers.

The notion of pupil empowerment is one which is often found difficult by therapists who have for so long worked within a medical model. Physiotherapists, for example, may see their role as interventionist, doing something to a patient in order to arrest further deterioration, or to overcome a debilitating condition. The move from this position to one in which pupils are encouraged to make their own decisions in terms of their personal management is profound. Staff who are moving along the pupil empowerment path need to be aware of this. They need to involve therapists in discussions which ensure that programmes designed for the medical wellbeing of pupils are not jeopardised, whilst at the same time encouraging therapists to move to integrate therapy programmes into group teaching situations. Encouraging therapists to share in the development of curriculum plans and the drawing up of school policy is one step towards overcoming these problems.

Conclusion

This chapter has demonstrated that there are many areas of curriculum management which need to be addressed by schools, and that these cannot be tackled overnight. Forward planning, and effective use of the school development plan provide a key to moving forward in this difficult area. These alone will be insufficient, however, unless they involve the whole school as a community. Governors, school staff, other professionals, parents, and most importantly pupils, all have responsibilities for the development and management of the curriculum. The effective school will be the one which incorporates all of these into its planning and monitoring processes.

Chapter Five

Redefining Personal and Social Development

Introduction

In chapter two we expanded upon the description of the whole curriculum given by National Curriculum Council in *Curriculum Guidance 3, The Whole Curriculum* (NCC, 1990a). This description states that:

> Section 1 of the Education Reform Act 1988 (ERA) places a statutory responsibility upon schools to provide a broad and balanced curriculum which
>
> - promotes the spiritual, moral, cultural, mental and physical development of pupils at the school and of society
> - prepares pupils for the opportunities, responsibilities and experiences of adult life. (p.1)

The description goes on to state that:

> The National Curriculum alone will not provide the necessary breadth, but the 10 subjects together with religious education (defined in the Act as the 'basic curriculum') can form the foundation. (p.1)

Upon the foundation provided by the basic curriculum, schools are required to build a whole curriculum which encompasses:

> additional subjects beyond the 10 subjects of the National Curriculum;
>
> an accepted range of cross-curricular elements;
>
> extra-curricular activities. (p. 1)

and which takes account of the 'intangibles which come from the spirit and ethos of each school.' In addition, the development of the whole curriculum should acknowledge:

the contribution to be made by deployment of:

the most effective teaching methods;

efficient and imaginative management of the curriculum and of the school. (NCC, 1990a, p.1)

In this book, we have explored the significance of this description for schools for pupils with learning difficulties - schools where honest attempts have been made to provide an education for the whole pupil. Chapter two dealt with some of the issues arising from the provision of access to curricular content for pupils with learning difficulties. Chapter three described some of the ways in which whole curriculum development might suggest revision of accepted practice in relation to teaching approaches and learning styles. Chapter four discussed the effective use of the structures available to the school team in managing curricular planning, curricular delivery, recording, reporting and assessment.

The task of this final chapter is to bring these issues together in order to create a coherent vision of a whole curriculum for pupils with learning difficulties - a curriculum which, in line with the Education Reform Act and the stated aims of many schools, truly promotes the balanced development of pupils and which prepares them for the realities of adult life.

This chapter will also seek to show that effective whole curriculum planning can be used to promote the personal and social development of pupils with learning difficulties - both through the considered implementation of a curriculum for personal and social education and through analysis of those aspects of the life of schools which can be referred to as the hidden curriculum. We will look briefly at some of the ways in which pupils' personal and social development has been viewed in mainstream schools and will consider the relevance of these models to pupils with learning difficulties.

Finally, this chapter will suggest that pupils' personal and social development will be enhanced by increased access to the whole curriculum on a number of levels. Thus school staff with a commitment to the effective implementation of courses of personal and social education will offer pupils access to an expanded breadth of curricular content. By employing a balanced range of teaching approaches which facilitate a variety of active learning styles, they will ensure that pupils have the possibility of access to the purpose and meaning of activities. Further, they will provide routes by which pupils may gain access to those structures which are created in order to manage the work of schools. We will suggest that the whole curriculum should be interpreted in ways which will empower pupils in preparation for their adult lives.

The whole pupil

A distinction between personal and social development and personal and social education is at the heart of our position in this book. Personal and social education appears on many timetables and often consists of work on self-help skills or, in mainstream schools, units on topics such as alcohol, sex and drugs. However effective these taught schemes of work might be, they contribute only partially to pupils' personal and social development. Our contention is that a concern with the personal and social development of pupils should permeate all aspects of the work of schools, including the nature of relationships between staff and pupils at every level. Our stance on personal and social development affects the three areas covered in the previous chapters: curricular content, teaching approaches and learning styles and management of the curriculum. Hence, after reading this chapter we hope you will start again - in order to reconsider content, teaching approaches and management issues.

The Whole Curriculum (NCC, 1990a, p.7) states that:

> the personal and social development of pupils is a major aim of education; personal and social education being the means by which this aim is achieved.

The suggestion is that access to a curriculum which includes programmes of personal and social education is an entitlement for all pupils from 5 to 16. Schools therefore need to consider creating policy statements and related schemes of work which will enable them to implement such programmes. The National Curriculum Council's own contribution to the process of developing the personal and social education curriculum comes in the form of the cross-curricular elements - the dimensions, skills and themes. NCC (1990a, p.2) does acknowledge, however, that

> it would be possible to construct a list of an almost infinite number of cross-curricular elements which taken together make a major contribution to personal and social education.

and that aspects of the basic curriculum will also be very relevant in terms of pupils' personal and social development. There is a great deal of room for manoeuvre within this description of the curriculum for personal and social education, offered within a description of the whole curriculum which (beyond the fact that the basic curriculum is defined in statute) is itself broad and flexible. The delineation of the cross-curricular elements which has so far been provided is partial. The *Curriculum Guidance* booklets *4* to *8* (NCC, 1990, b-f) offer an exploration of 'five themes which, although by no means a conclusive list, seem to most people to be pre-eminent'. Perhaps school staff will wish to explore additional themes as part of their teaching programmes.

Curriculum Guidance 3 (NCC, 1990a) provides a brief description of the dimensions in terms of equal opportunities and a bare list of core skills which is not intended to be exhaustive. School staff may wish to expand and elaborate these ideas also. Certainly schools will continue to offer 'additional subjects' beyond the basic curriculum and to provide opportunities for extra-curricular activities. Given the acknowledgement of pupils' personal and social development as a 'major aim of education', there is clearly much for schools to develop for themselves within a broad and relatively unprescribed area.

How all of this material is to be taught is left up to schools. *The Whole Curriculum* (NCC, 1990a, p.7) asserts that

> it is the birthright of the teaching profession, and must always remain so, to decide on the best and most appropriate means of imparting education to pupils.

Similarly, there are as yet no statutory restrictions upon the strategies and structures which schools employ in creating the spirit and ethos which is seen as making an intangible contribution to the personal and social development of pupils.

There is also, as yet, no statutory restriction upon the ways in which schools might define the whole pupil who is to be developed by the whole curriculum. In listing the 'physical, sexual, moral, social and vocational' selves (NCC, 1990a) which are the concern of the present set of five cross-curricular themes, National Curriculum Council is drawing upon the ideas of Wall (1974), Hamblin (1978; 1981) and Watkins (1989). Expanding upon an original concept of Wall's, these authors of seminal works in the arena of personal and social education have between them generated a set of seven selves all of which need to be taken into account in consideration of the whole pupil and her development. These selves comprise:

- the bodily, or physical, self;
- the sexual self;
- the social self;
- the vocational self;
- the moral/political self;
- the self as learner and
- the self in the organisation.

School staff have argued that even this set of selves fails to acknowledge all the aspects of selfhood with which schools need to concern themselves if they are to become involved with the development of the whole pupil. Some people, for instance, feel that distinctions should be drawn between the moral, philosophical and spiritual development of pupils. Others suggest that there is such a thing as a cognitive, or intellectual self – the self of ideas, concepts and understandings. Again, it can be claimed that schools have a duty to take account of an emotional self, helping pupils to come to terms with their feelings, particularly, perhaps, in relation to their social and sexual identities.

What is clear is that selfhood is a complex phenomenon and that the National Curriculum Council does not claim to have provided adequate guidance with regard to the development of the whole pupil. This task remains the responsibility of schools and their staff teams and, although daunting, it is a task which school staff should accept with enthusiasm. In many senses it represents a devolution of responsibility for the most significant aspects of the education of pupils with learning difficulties to the school community and leaves professionals, governors, parents and pupils with a relatively free hand in defining a whole curriculum which is truly relevant to the development of particular groups of individual pupils. The seven selves framework does suggest, however, that the varied curricular models which individual school communities adopt should all facilitate the development of the whole pupil within the flexibility of the whole curriculum.

The goal of education

School staff who assert that their main aim is to develop their pupils' potential must ensure that the individual nature of pupils' learning is respected. In the past this may simply have meant that schools, in seeking to develop pupils' autonomy, would implement a range of programmes designed to train pupils in practical independence or self-help skills. Carpenter (1992) argues that such goals need to be retained and yet extended if the curriculum is to offer pupils 'maximum personal autonomy'. Increasingly there is a groundswell of opinion which proposes that autonomy is about much more than the ability to tie shoe laces or make cups of coffee. Phrases such as 'self-reliance', 'self-esteem' or 'self-confidence', drawn from the argot of professionals concerned with the personal and social development of pupils in mainstream settings, suggest that this opinion is correct. These phrases are redolent of something more than mere pragmatic competency in terms of day to day functioning. They suggest that autonomous individuals should have a sense that they want a cup of coffee, perhaps in preference to the cup of tea which is being offered; that they have a right to state that preference; that they deserve a cup of coffee; and then, should their preference still not be acted upon by others, that they have the will and the skills necessary to make or purchase a cup of coffee for themselves.

One dictionary defines autonomy as 'the right or state of self government' and as 'the freedom to determine one's own actions, behaviour, etc.' This definition echoes the words of Carl Rogers in describing the self-actualising or fully functioning person (Rogers, 1983, p.276):

> The free person moves out voluntarily, freely, responsibly, to play her significant part in a world whose determined events move through her and through her spontaneous choice and will.

Rogers offers this description in contrast to the scientific, deterministic analysis of the individual and her place in the world given by Skinner in establishing a rationale for behaviourism (Skinner, 1953, p.477):

> The hypothesis that man is not free is essential to the application of scientific method to the study of human behaviour. The free inner man who is held responsible for his behaviour is only a prescientific substitute for the kinds of causes which are discovered in the course of scientific analysis. All these alternative causes lie outside the individual.

Roger's position is not simply, in Skinner's terms, prescientific. He acknowledges both the determined nature of external events and the freedom and responsibility of the individual. He does not seek to deny that people need skills in order to act within the real world, nor that people act and react in response to conditions and experiences in the world around them. He does, however, contend that the individual can develop the will to choose if she is given the opportunity to grasp the meaning behind acts of decision-making and the confidence to deal with consequences which choosing demands.

The aims of the self-advocacy movement, People First (Bourlet, 1990), mirror Rogers' views rather than those of Skinner. People with learning difficulties are themselves arguing for a community within which they can act as freely functioning persons in society rather than as persons upon whom society imposes its conditions. This is not to argue that pupils do not need to be prepared for life in the adult world or that society does not have valid expectations of the education system in terms of equipping pupils to make their contribution within a broader system of structures and responsibilities. But the goals of social acceptability or vocational adaptability are clearly inadequate ones if schools are to offer pupils the chance to develop towards true autonomy. Autonomy, in Rogers' view and increasingly in the view of people with learning difficulties themselves, implies active, self-determined participation on the part of the individual within her community.

Mainstream models

This view raises issues about the values, ethics and spirit which inform the work of schools. School communities, professionals, governors, parents and pupils acting together, and the individual members of those communities, need to continue to ask questions about the purpose of education. The National Curriculum may have prescribed the content of a basic curriculum. It has not resolved definitively the major questions posed by the Education Reform Act of 1988: how to promote the 'spiritual, moral, cultural, mental and physical development of pupils at the school and of society' and how to prepare pupils for the 'opportunities, responsibilities and experiences of adult life'.

If there is a continuum of intent between the aim of individual liberation (education to free each person to reach her full potential by challenging and questioning established codes) and societal benefit (education for vocational utility or social conformity), then each school will need to find its own place upon it – a position where these potentially conflicting aims are in a satisfactory state of balance. Each school will need to seek its own mandate for its position, taking account of statutory requirements and the recommendations of official guidance, but also seeking consensus among professionals, governors, parents and local communities. Increasingly the pursuit of consensus will also entail listening to the views of pupils and their representatives. Each school will need to ensure that the model of adulthood for which it is preparing its pupils remains both realistic and contemporary, avoiding a complacent dependence upon outmoded historical stereotypes while eschewing dogma-driven heroic idealism.

Staff concerned with personal and social education in mainstream schools have been grappling with these sorts of issues for some years. It may therefore be instructive to look at some of the paradigms which inform their practice. From its original conceptualisation in the 1970s, personal and social education has been a school-led, teacher-driven initiative. It first received official recognition when Her Majesty's Inspectorate published *A View of the Curriculum* (DES, 1980b). Developments in schools continued, fuelled by initiatives like TVEI and Records of Achievement (McLaughlin, 1990). The National Curriculum Council, as we have seen, formally acknowledged the role of personal and social education in 1990 in *Curriculum Guidance 3 : The Whole Curriculum*. During this twenty year history, a body of theoretical literature has emerged and this now offers an opportunity for retrospective analysis.

Ryder and Campbell (1988) suggest that there have been at least four models for personal and social education operating in mainstream schools over recent years. The first of these, which they call the 'Pastoral/Individual' model, represents an agenda for pupil-centred personal liberation. In this model the teacher, who has the role of an empathic facilitator or counsellor, seeks to encourage self-awareness in pupils leading to effective inter-personal relationships. The methodology is characterised by group work, with pupils engaged as active participants in the learning process. Pupil experiences are further valued and validated by means of individual guidance or counselling sessions. The aim of the teacher is to foster pupil self-esteem and self-empowerment.

Ryder and Campbell's second model can also be seen as a pupil-centred empowerment model but it focuses more upon rationality and understanding than upon empathy and feelings. Ryder and Campbell call this the 'Educational/Rational' model and suggest that the teacher, in the role of arbitrator, seeks to provide access to intellectual and practical resources, fostering understanding through the exemplification and development of the power of reason. The intention is that a liberating initiation into public forms of knowledge takes place through abstract discussions and debates in which pupils are theoretically active.

The third model which Ryder and Campbell describe could be seen as having as its aim the creation of a better society. In the 'Radical/Political' model, young people are encouraged to engage in social and political analysis by a teacher who acts as an energiser, prompting pupils to explore their sense of social justice. Through group problem solving, a sense of community and of respect for self and others is fostered. Pupils undertake active research as collaborators, making explicit links between personal experiences and socio-political structures. The aim is to equip pupils for the critical analysis of social situations and issues, encouraging them to recognise and question power structures, oppression and prejudice.

Finally Ryder and Campbell identify a 'Medical/Transitional' model which seeks to promote economic and social efficiency by pre-empting deviancy. In this model the teacher has the role of expert, controlling the transmission of relevant, objective knowledge and the progress of pupils towards appropriate, perhaps approved, adult behaviour. The pupils assimilate given content as passive recipients, moving towards increased social and vocational competence. The aim is to foster an awareness in pupils which will promote conformity to social norms, mores and roles.

Contrast and compare

Ryder and Campbell do not suggest that any one of these models represents an entirely adequate version of the curriculum for personal and social education. Each of them, however, reveals something of what personal and social education has, in reality, been about in mainstream schools in the same way that the stances described in chapter one of this volume reveal something of the history of teacher-learner relationships in schools for pupils with learning difficulties. Interestingly there appear to be many parallels.

For example, the deficit models described in chapter one are very similar to Ryder and Campbell's medical/transitional model. Both stances reveal attitudes in the teacher which identify deficits in the pupil; which regard pupils as aggregations of problems which stand in need of remediation. Both models cast teachers in the role of trainer, equipping pupils with ways of behaving which conform to social norms. In both models the objective is to work towards pupil competency by relying upon the teacher's expert awareness of appropriate adult target behaviours. In both models the long term aim is to produce an efficient, wholesome society free of deviant behaviours and the problems which these cause. Neither of these approaches to teaching seek to put pupils on the road to autonomy as we have defined it here. They tend, on the contrary, to view pupils as inherently faulty. The teacher's job is to recondition pupils so that they will function properly in society.

The caring/needs aspect of the deficit models identified in chapter one echoes Ryder and Campbell's pastoral/individual model. Both approaches are ostensibly pupil-centred, focusing upon the perceived needs of individual pupils. However, where the mainstream model emphasises an enabling empathy which will help to empower the pupil, staff in schools for pupils with learning difficulties have often offered a form of care which can become smothering and promote and prolong dependency. Preconceptions about 'eternal children' and 'handicapped people' who will 'always need help' characterise this well-intentioned but not always very liberating form of caring. Again, with the best of intentions, parents, relatives, and even some of the voluntary organisations which exist to champion the interests of people with learning difficulties, have often tended to perpetuate the culture within which the caring/needs model can thrive.

Again, schools for pupils with learning difficulties have their own form of didactic stance, parallel to the educational/rational teaching model identified by Ryder and Campbell in mainstream schools. This approach identifies the task of teachers as being to fill pupils, seen as empty vessels, with skills, knowledge and understanding. This stance, like many of the others, locates all the expertise and most of the power firmly within the teacher. Interestingly, the National Curriculum has been seen in many schools for pupils with learning difficulties as creating a need for this form of teaching – almost as if some of that expertise and power were now located outside schools and within central government, putting teachers in the role merely of conduits between the sources of knowledge and the pupils as passive recipients. Certainly there is a tension within this sort of approach between a pupil-centred 'education for all' philosophy and a perception that somehow the manipulation of the curriculum has a great deal to do with a movement towards economic and social efficiency.

Finally, there have been parallels in schools for pupils with learning difficulties with mainstream radical/political teaching models. We could group these usefully under the heading of partnership stances since they all have some measure of pupil-teacher dialogue about control sharing as a characteristic. Experiments with intensive interaction (Nind and Hewett, 1988), gentle teaching (McGee et al, 1987), group work (Rose, 1991) and pupil participation in the learning process (Smith, 1987; Tilstone, 1991) have all introduced styles of teaching which emphasise partnership and dialogue into schools for pupils with learning difficulties. Many of these initiatives have been driven by a sense of political, social or humanistic justice, but, perhaps unlike their mainstream counterparts, they have focused firmly upon the liberation of the individual as a part of the process of societal change.

A discussion of these approaches, stances and models at some length has served to reinforce a historical perspective and to indicate some of the common territory between mainstream schools and schools for pupils with learning difficulties. It has also, as the following sections will show, served to introduce many of the key issues which must be addressed in any analysis of personal and social development. The discussion has introduced many of the ideas around which personal and social education is centred and indicated some of the models for personal and social education which are to be considered as inadequate.

It is clear that courses of personal and social education cannot be adequately described solely in terms of curricular content, whether that content comprises checklists of self-help and independence skills or a 'pot pourri' (Pring, 1984) of topics such as those proposed by the National Curriculum's collection of themes. Of course, there is content within the curriculum for personal and social education, but not only content. Similarly, there is a sense in which personal and social education has a great deal to do with the remediation of pupils' personal and social problems. However, as a curriculum, it cannot be seen only as an elaborate form of emotional first aid or as an extension of the role of the school nurse.

Hopefully the above discussions have indicated that planning for personal and social education entails consideration of teaching approaches, learning styles and management structures. But pupils' personal and social development will not be assured through relationships and classroom processes alone, however committed to pupil power the teacher as political crusader or would-be counsellor may be. Finally, the curriculum for personal and social education should not be seen as a 'catch all' curriculum – a convenient category into which to pop all those troublesome school activities which teachers wish to retain but which refuse to fit neatly into any of the headings offered by the core and other foundation subjects of the National Curriculum. The curriculum for personal and social education must be considered, structured and planned like any other aspect of the curriculum. As these discussions have indicated, however, the development of a curriculum for personal and social education may suggest a fundamental review of certain aspects of the work of some schools.

Power and control

Before moving on to look at some of the ways in which personal and social education may usefully be conceptualised within the whole curriculum, it may be worth pausing to examine some of the important issues which have arisen from the discussions so far. Most of these issues revolve around the nature of the central power relationship between teacher and pupil. Broadly it is the contention of this chapter that the medical, psychological and remedial foundations of much of the work carried out in schools for pupils with learning difficulties have left a legacy of relationships in which the professionals see themselves as rightfully holding the power. Just as the medical profession is today having to come to terms with patients who are seeking a form of health care in which information and responsibility for courses of treatment are more openly shared, so teachers in schools for pupils with learning difficulties may find themselves needing to reformulate the kinds of relationships which they have with their pupils.

In essence, there is a question here about how school staff see the purpose of their work. Do schools exist in order to empower individual pupils or in order to bolster a system of societal control? It is worth noting that some of the mainstream models we looked at earlier deliberately seek to liberate individuals and to encourage them to challenge and question forms of authority and control. For the most part, only the partnership model among the stances characterising work in schools for pupils with learning difficulties appears to have an element of this spirit. School staff need to decide whether this is a matter of deliberate policy and an aspect of their work which they wish to retain, or whether this is simply an unchallenged hangover from non-educational regimes.

Medical and psychological models for the education of pupils with learning difficulties originate from a position which suggests that professionals possess the knowledge which permits diagnosis, prognosis, prescription and cure and that the destiny of individual persons is conditioned by inherited characteristics and by culture and experience. This position can be compounded in situations in which attitudes towards pupils with learning difficulties acknowledge the 'needs', the 'problems', the 'handicaps' and the 'difficulties' rather than the people themselves.

The concept of progress in schools for pupils with learning difficulties has entailed notions about 'remediation' and 'normalisation' rather than empowerment and liberation. The aim of many schools has been to steer pupils away from idiosyncracy and deviancy towards 'socially acceptable' codes of behaviour, defined, generally speaking, by professionals. School cultures have tended to put power into the hands of professionals, as part of a working partnership with parents. As noted earlier, this partnership can, in practice, disempower pupils by perpetuating an ethos of dependency.

If this seems like an outrageous statement, consider all three aspects of the education process which we have discussed in this book so far. Curriculum content is controlled, if not from the centre then certainly by professionals, governors and parents. Schools for pupils with learning difficulties which offer anything more than token timetable options for older pupils are indeed a rarity. Teaching methods also tend to perpetuate a system of teacher control. Even the new version of the EDY materials (Farrell et al, 1992) deals with concepts like 'prompting', 'shaping' and 'using rewards', all selected by the teacher or trainer. Access to structures such as the school development plan tends to be limited to those on upper rungs of the professional hierarchy. Pupils are commonly not active participants in their own annual review and in many schools the full significance of pupil empowerment entailed in the records of achievement process has yet to be realised. Many of these structures were also discussed in chapter four.

If the sharing of power with pupils is a rarity on this macro level, and many professionals and parents would argue that the disabilities of pupils mean that any attempt at power sharing on this level would inevitably be tokenistic or demeaning, can we assume that schools for pupils with learning difficulties make strenuous efforts to ensure that plenty of opportunities exist for pupils to practise and exercise self-responsibility in more modest ways? A brief look at some of the sub-structures which tend to obtain at the micro level in schools for pupils with learning difficulties would suggest that this is not the case.

Rules, routines and rituals

All schools have rules, routines and rituals in some form or another. Some rules are designed to ensure pupil safety (for example, the exhortation not to run in the corridor); some routines provide a sense of social responsibility in microcosm (for example, tidying up the library); some rituals help to create a genuine sense of corporate identity (for example, the celebration of individual achievement during assembly). There are many examples of rules, routines and rituals which have sound ideological origins but which become self-perpetuating and meaningless, or even counter-productive, for pupils. Ultimately such structures simply become sources of stability or comfort for staff and turn into symbols of control.

School staff would acknowledge, for instance, the need to provide structured sessions in order to begin to teach pupils that Makaton signs can convey meaning. The aim, however, must be to encourage pupils to sign spontaneously. A stage will be reached at which the timetabled lessons may impede pupil progress towards conversational signing. Pupils may come to depend upon the prompt of a pre-ordained signing opportunity and see these as the only situations in which they are required to sign.

Many examples of other such regimes, which actually generate dependency upon prompts, or certain members of staff or certain bits of equipment, exist and stand in need of re-examination. All such rules, routines and rituals can be tested against the question: 'Whose needs does this structure really serve?' Those that perpetuate unhelpful patterns of control and dependency can be set aside.

Help and guidance

Again, all schools seek to provide help and guidance. There is a difference, however, between guidance which is offered and help which is given whether or not it is requested or required. Again, the origins of such help may be entirely benevolent. Staff wish to be caring. The very notion of 'difficulty' suggests to many warm-hearted people the charitable idea of help.

As many who are elderly or disabled know, however, help can be unwanted. It can create an unpleasant sense of powerlessness as the helper takes control of the situation and of the help victim. Pupils with learning difficulties may be over-helped in this way by well-meaning professionals and family members. They may become dependent upon help, and be denied opportunities to learn and grow through solving their own problems and exploring failure. Those of us who cast ourselves in the role of helping constantly need to re-examine our motives. Who needs the helping act most – the person experiencing the difficulties or the helper? Why does the helper need to help – how important to the helper is the power which helping entails?

Even the concept of guidance has a significant subtext – the professional knows best and will channel social and moral inadequates in approved directions. The use of help and guidance needs to be challenged most particularly in situations where clients appear to be most dependent. Vigilance is required in order to ensure that support is available at all times but that unnecessary help is never imposed.

Hierarchies

Many institutions operate on a hierarchical basis and hierarchies can provide a model of control. Thus, headteachers have power over teachers who have power over classroom assistants who have power over voluntary helpers who have power over pupils. It is inevitable that pupils tend to be at the bottom of this kind of hierarchy. The situation can be exacerbated by checklists and developmental hierarchies which highlight inadequacies and deficits in those pupils and which serve to emphasise a quasi-scientific rationale for their lowly status.

Hierarchies do not have to be oppressive. They can be consultative and collaborative, with power being exercised on a delegated basis, responsibly and purposefully. Again, vigilance needs to be exercised in order to ensure that hierarchical power is not wielded for its own sake or simply because those who are controlled tend to wish to exert control over those who are perceived as being lower down the pecking order.

Praise, reward and punishment

Praise implies power; rewards and punishments are symbols of that power. Those with situational control can say: 'If you do what I want, I will approve of you. I will tell you that you are a good boy or girl. I may give you a hug or give you a sweet. But if you fail to do what I want I will withhold my approval, take away your privileges, or even deny you contact with your friends.' This power may not necessarily imply any sinister motivation.

Indeed, staff working among pupils with learning difficulties have been told that pupil progress may depend upon generous praise and the judicious use of rewards and sanctions. Those who employ incentives and disincentives beyond the pupil's own motivation to learn or to succeed should be aware of the power pattern which they are establishing. Perhaps they should be prepared to diversify their monopoly over the control of praise, rewards and punishments by encouraging pupil self-assessment, peer group assessment, or even pupil evaluation of staff effectiveness.

An honest exploration of these discussion points in specific school settings may provoke some profound reassessments of the foundations of work with pupils with learning difficulties. Do schools exist in order to support individual pupils in their progress towards adult autonomy or in order to prepare pupils to conform to the expectations of a society which is likely to have little understanding of, or empathy with, the lives of people with disabilities? What is the true nature of the relationship between pupils and staff? Is there a sense in which the interpersonal power structures which exist in schools for pupils with learning difficulties deny the possibility of real pupil autonomy even as the rhetoric proclaims this as the goal of education?

Another way?

It is possible that the stance proposed by this chapter will suggest a reformulation of the relationships between pupils and staff and a reconstitution of school aims and ethos. This section will provide a theoretical basis for this endeavour and a structure which may help schools to work towards a new formula for the education of pupils with learning difficulties.

In essence this new formula must take as its starting point the idea that education is about liberation and that persons with learning difficulties are no less capable of attaining autonomy than anyone else. We have already contrasted, in an earlier section of this chapter, the views of Skinner and Rogers with respect to the concept of free will, and have noted that it has been the behavioural, deterministic, Skinnerian view which has tended to inform the teaching of pupils with learning difficulties over the years. Paulo Friere, in his book *Pedagogy of the Oppressed* (Friere, 1972, p.23), has more to say about the notion of conditioning and prescriptive education:

> One of the basic elements of the relationship between oppressor and oppressed is prescription. Every prescription represents the imposition of one man's choice upon another, transforming the consciousness of the man prescribed to into one that conforms to the prescriber's consciousness.

Friere goes on to describe a form of problem-solving education, characterised by dialogue between teacher and learner, which he identifies as being designed to liberate the individual rather than to perpetuate forms of oppression. He states that:

> Authentic education is not carried on by A for B or by A about B, but rather by A with B, mediated by the world.   (p.66)

Friere argues that teachers need to enter into a genuine state of solidarity with their students – a state which echoes the empathy identified by Rogers as an essential prerequisite for giving students the freedom to learn (Rogers,

1983). The concepts of solidarity and empathy were adopted by the proponents of Gentle Teaching (McGee et al, 1987) and Intensive Interaction (Nind and Hewett, 1988) in their attempts to break down the culture of teacher superiority, teacher domination and teacher prescription which has characterised the work of schools for pupils with learning difficulties over the years. These writers would argue that staff need to shed the 'us and them' mentality which still subtly permeates the culture of many such schools.

These views are finding increasing support. In their chapter on 'Annual Reviews: An Active Partnership', Hughes and Carpenter (1991, p.219-220) state that:

> The ownership of the curriculum must be shared. Indeed Circular 22/89 emphasises the place of the pupil in contributing to the Annual Review procedure. Increasingly, through wider opportunities and raised expectations, young people with SLD are proving themselves capable of effective decision making in relation to their own life goals.

Tilstone, in her chapter 'Pupils' Views', (Tilstone, 1991), argues that teachers must listen to and respect the views of their pupils without seeking constantly to instruct, channel and dominate. She also argues for a new form of relationship between teacher and pupil – a relationship which will be characterised by collaboration and which can find expression within the records of achievement process:

> Records of Achievement require a teacher to change her role: from judge to witness; from provider of information to provider of opportunity; from director to partner; from authority figure to consultant; from instructor to counsellor. (Tilstone, 1991, p. 37)

Interestingly, both Hughes and Carpenter, and Tilstone identify existing school structures (annual review and records of achievement) as vehicles for the delivery of their radical reformulation of the teacher/pupil relationship. The remainder of this chapter will seek to find other ways in which existing school policy can be modified and revitalised in order to provide liberating whole person education for pupils with learning difficulties.

In an earlier section of this chapter we discussed a wide-ranging definition of the whole curriculum which appeared to offer plenty of scope for the development of a curriculum for liberation and autonomy. The work of Hughes and Carpenter and Tilstone, among others, indicates that there is room within existing structures for a new spirit and for a reformulation of the concept of whole person education. One possible framework for such a reformulation has been offered by Best (1989) in his description of a new model for whole person education in mainstream settings. Best describes a model of curriculum development which takes account of all the aspects of the whole curriculum identified at the start of this chapter and which brings together many of the issues raised in this volume. The model is given in Figure 7.

Within the category of **Curriculum** Best examines the needs of the pupil, the child as a learner. He argues that curriculum planning should ensure that pupils have access to the content of the curriculum and to the concepts, facts, knowledge and understanding as well as the skills which they will need in adult life. Pupils should also have opportunities to develop new attitudes to life and to learning through teaching approaches which encourage a variety of effective learning styles. Considering the work of Rogers (1983) and Friere (1972), as well as some of the characteristics of personal and social education identified by Ryder and Campbell (1988), alongside the arguments put forward in chapter three of this book it might be possible to identify some of the characteristics of learning which could be said to be effective in terms of pupils' personal and social development. Effective learning opportunities will be those which:

- are relevant to pupils' day to day reality and have a clear meaning and purpose for them;
- take account of pupils' interests, aptitudes, experiences and skills and engage the whole pupil;
- are interactive, encouraging exploration and problem solving through partnership and dialogue between peers and between pupils and teachers;
- are intrinsically motivating, promoting pupil initiation and facilitating self-assessment through shared performance criteria.

Best's analysis of **Casework** encourages school staff to consider the needs of the child for security, warmth, guidance, patience, support and love. Best suggests that these aspects of the whole curriculum will be developed through meaningful individual relationships between staff and pupils – relationships which extend beyond the guidance tutorial and which express the kind of respect, empathy and solidarity which we discussed in earlier paragraphs.

The **Control** element of Best's model represents an attempt to meet the needs of the citizen for an orderly environment, for rules and for sanctions, but also for a sense of participation and belonging which suggests a philosophy of collaboration and power sharing. Best's vision of control is democratic and offers pupils access to and active roles within decision-making and disciplinary structures and processes.

Best argues that the task of **Management** is to facilitate all of the above by meeting the needs of staff for leadership, training, appraisal, appreciation, resources, inspiration and so forth as discussed in chapter four. Only

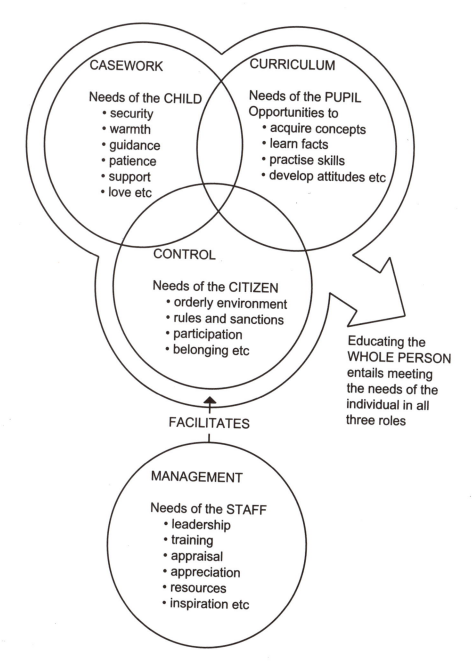

Figure 7: A 'whole person' model for personal and social education (Best, 1989)

when school staff are effectively meeting the needs of pupils in all three interlinked areas can they claim to be educating the whole person. It follows that any effective curriculum for personal and social development will also need to take account of all these aspects.

One brief example may serve to illustrate some of Best's arguments. Suppose that one of the priorities identified within the school development plan of a school for pupils with learning difficulties concerns the development of schemes of work in relation to pupils' vocational selves as one of the seven areas of selfhood suggested within the 'Whole Pupil' section earlier in this chapter. Best's model might suggest that the relevant curriculum content should be identified. Clearly the themes of careers education and guidance and education for economic and industrial understanding will contain much of the relevant material although staff may also wish to consider the contribution which the geography and history programmes of study could make to this area of development. Best's model further suggests that the schemes of work should detail an appropriate range of teaching approaches which will provide pupils with effective learning opportunities. These may include some classroom sessions with videos or visiting speakers; some role play sessions; a mini-enterprise project; lots of visits – to real places of work or to industrial museums and work experience placements. Hopefully the pupils themselves might be encouraged to identify the visits they wish to make and to plan their own methods of information gathering.

The casework aspect of Best's model will indicate a need to provide individual counselling and guidance sessions for pupils as they contemplate their options for future employment or occupation. School staff will be able to provide pupils with information about interesting work places to visit and help pupils anticipate some of the differences between school and a work experience placement. It is quite likely that these discussions will open up other areas of aspiration or concern for the pupils involved and staff will need to be prepared to support pupils in coping with their own emotional responses to these issues. Visits from careers officers; the monitoring of pupils on work experience and awareness raising trips out to potential future placements will also need to be planned.

The school's own structures could be adapted to make a contribution to pupils' vocational education. Clocking in and signing off procedures could be implemented; younger pupils might be given work-style responsibilities around the school; pupils could be encouraged to make their journeys to and from school independently on public transport; participants in School Council meetings could take on the roles of union negotiators or boards of directors. Through all of this, the school's management team will have to ensure that there are adequate opportunities for staff development through INSET opportunities, for instance, or through teacher placements in industry and that minibus availability and supply cover permit the range of group visits and individual teacher journeys which the schemes of work encompass.

Conclusion

In this book we have attempted to discuss many of the ways in which staff can ensure that pupils have meaningful access to all the aspects of the whole curriculum identified in Best's model. We have examined the issues which surround curriculum content, especially the notion of entitlement and access to the knowledge, skills and understanding which comprise a curriculum for all. We have paid particular attention to the relationship between the themes, skills and dimensions, identified by Carpenter (1992) as the 'bedrock' of the curriculum; additional subjects and the core and other foundation subjects.

We have described a range of teaching approaches and learning styles, including problem solving and groupwork, and argued for a considered policy of variety and balance. Teaching approaches and learning styles have a significant contribution to make to pupils' personal and social development. They should facilitate pupil understanding, involvement, participation and initiation. Consideration should be given to the messages which are passed to pupils through staff attitudes as a form of hidden curriculum.

We have described some of the structures to which pupils might be given access in order to permit participation in rule setting and systems of control. Records of achievement procedures and the annual review process have been identified as reasonable places to begin but a curriculum for democracy in action encompassing self advocacy, peer group advocacy and student councils might also suggest that pupils could be afforded access to disciplinary procedures, to rule making structures and to the school development planning process.

Finally we have indicated that none of this will mean very much in real terms unless relationships between staff and pupils change at a basic level. Friere (1972, p.26) says:

> The oppressor shows solidarity with the oppressed only when he stops regarding the oppressed as an abstract category and sees them as persons who have been unjustly dealt with.

Friere asks teachers to learn to see the world as their students see it and to enter into a problem solving dialogue with their students as 'critical co-investigators'. Taken together with the comments we have made about access to curriculum content; about policy with regard to a range of teaching and learning styles and about the democratisation of school structures, we consider that we have identified an agenda for the redefinition of the whole curriculum as a curriculum for liberation.

Implications

If this interpretation of the concept of the whole curriculum is to be meaningfully implemented it will imply some profound changes in the ways that many schools make provision for pupils with learning difficulties. Staff will need to develop new kinds of relationships with their pupils. Pupils may be given access to organisational structures which have been regarded hitherto as the territory of senior management. Schemes of work will expand to encompass new areas of knowledge and understanding. Staff will need to develop their classroom and time management skills in order to take account of a broader range of teaching approaches and learning styles. There will be a great need for staff development. School managers will be required to acknowledge the necessity for awareness raising and consciousness shifting among staff and parents alike. There will be a need for systems of mutual support which will demand an approach based upon the commitment of the whole school community.

This will be a movement in which school staff and managers will need to work in concert. While some initiatives, not only from within education, such as The Children Act (1989), will be seen to endorse the concepts of pupil consultation and involvement in the decision making processes, there will be other bodies of opinion which will seek to reverse tendencies towards reform along the lines we have identified. School governors will, of course, need to be persuaded of the wisdom of the proposed changes. Other professionals who work among pupils with learning difficulties alongside teaching staff may well come from institutional cultures which continue to minimise the client's right to expect consultation and participation. Some parents may fail to see the need to share the annual review process with their sons and daughters, particularly if the expressed expectations and aspirations of the young people involved differ from their own. School staff may find themselves with a difficult path to tread between the acknowledged rights of parents and the potential expectations of pupils.

We would not wish to minimise the complexities or difficulties which the redefinition proposed in these pages will entail. It is our intention to provide evidence of the possibility of overcoming many of these obstacles in a second volume. This book will seek to illustrate ways in which the personal and social development of pupils with learning difficulties may be assured within a redefined whole curriculum and will be devoted largely to worked examples drawn from school practice. Meanwhile, it should be encouraging for school staff to realise that the changes we propose are in line with the views of the service users, special school survivors, as expressed by Simone Aspis (1991, p. 21):

> The whole school system seemed to be about control, containment and conformity. It was not about setting goals for children or helping them reach their full potential. I suppose I was rebellious but frustration must find an outlet when people condemn you to narrow horizons.
>
> Teachers never asked us what we wanted out of life. Perhaps that was because there wasn't much they thought we could do. There was no pupil involvement in school decisions like at other schools... Unlike mainstream schools, they didn't try to build upon what you could do, just accentuate what you couldn't. Children entering special education feel they are failures, but they are made even greater failures because of the policy of building on disability rather than ability.
>
> There is an assumption that the disabled person's greatest hurdle to a 'normal' life is the prejudice of the able-bodied community. But I have found the attitudes of special schools and the organisations specialising in services for the disabled the greatest obstacle... If anything is to change, the system must start listening to its users, develop education that will stretch pupils and involve those with disabilities in decision-making.

References

Ainscow, M. and Muncey, J. (1984) *SNAP*. Cardiff: Drake Educational Associates.

Ainscow, M. (1989) 'How should we respond to individual needs?', In: Ainscow, M. and Florek, A. (eds) *Special Educational Needs: Towards a Whole School Approach*. London: Fulton & National Council for Special Education.

Alexander, R., Rose, J. and Woodhead, C. (1992) *Curriculum Organisation and Classroom Practice in Primary Schools*. London: HMSO.

Ashdown, R., Carpenter, B. and Bovair, K. (eds)(1991) *The Curriculum Challenge: Access to the National Curriculum for Pupils with Learning Difficulties*. London: Falmer.

Aspis, S. (1991) 'The school never believed in us', *Viewpoint* in the *Education Independent*, 11 April 1991.

Batty P., Moon R. and Roaf C. (1987) 'Changing the curriculum at Peers', *British Journal of Special Education*, 14, (4), 170-1.

Bennett, N., Desforges, C., Cockburn, A. and Wilkinson B. (1984) *The Quality of Pupil Learning Experiences*. New Jersey: Lawrence Erlbaum Associates.

Bennett, N. and Cass, A. (1988) 'The effects of group composition on group interactive processes and pupil understanding', *British Educational Research Journal*, 15, (1), 19-32.

Bennett, N. (1991) 'The quality of classroom learning experiences for children with special educational needs'. In Ainscow, M. (ed) *Effective Schools for All*. London: Fulton.

Berger, M. (1982) 'Applied behaviour analysis in education: a critical assessment and some implications for training teachers', *Educational Psychology*, 2, 289-300.

Best, R. (1989) 'Pastoral care: some reflections and a re-statement', *Pastoral Care*, 7, (4), 7-13.

Biklen, D. (1990) 'Communication unbound: autism and praxis', *Harvard Educational Review*, 60, 291-314.

Biklen, D., Morton, M.W., Saha, S.N., Duncan, J., Gold, D., Hardardottir, M., Karna, E., O'Connor, S. and Rao, S. (1991) '"I AMN NOT A UTISTIVC ON THJE TYP" ("I'm not autistic on the typewriter")', *Disability, Handicap and Society*, 6, 161-180.

Billinge, R. (1988) 'The objectives model of curriculum development: a creaking bandwagon?', *Mental Handicap*, 16, 26-29.

Bourlet, G. (1990) 'Gary Bourlet speaks out', *Values into Action Newsletter*, 62, 7.

Brennan, W.K. (1974) *Shaping the Education of Slow Learners*. London: Routledge and Kegan Paul.

Byers, R. (1990) 'Topics: from myths to objectives', *British Journal of Special Education*, 17, (3), 109-112.

Carnine, D. (1977) 'Direct Instruction - DISTAR', In: Haring, H.G. and Bateman, B. (eds) *Teaching the Learning Disabled Child*. Englewood Cliffs, NJ: Prentice Hall.

Carpenter, B. (1992) 'The Whole Curriculum: Meeting the Needs of the Whole Child', In: Bovair, K., Carpenter B. and Upton G. (eds) *Special Curricula Needs*. London: Fulton.

Children Act, The (1989) CH 41 London: HMSO.

Conner, C. (ed)(1988) *Topic and Thematic Work in the Primary and Middle Years*. Cambridge: Cambridge Institute of Education.

DES (1978) *Special Educational Needs: Report of the Committee of Enquiry into the Education of Handicapped Children and Young People*. London: HMSO.

DES (1980a) *Education 5-9*. London: HMSO.

DES (1980b) *A View of the Curriculum*. London: HMSO.

DES (1984) *The Organisation and Content of the Curriculum in Special Schools*. London: HMSO.

DES (1989a) *A Survey of Provision for Pupils with Emotional/Behavioural Difficulties in Maintained Special Schools and Units*. A Report by HM Inspectors, London: HMSO.

DES (1989b) *Educating Physically Disabled Pupils*. A Report by HM Inspectors, London: HMSO.

DES (1989c) *Planning for School Development: Advice to Governors, Headteachers and Teachers*. London: HMSO.

DES (1991) *The Education Reform Act 1988: National Curriculum: Mathematics and Science Orders under Section 4. Circular No. 17/91*. London: HMSO.

DES (1992) *Technology Key Stages 1, 2 and 3*. A Report by HM Inspectors, London: HMSO.

East Sussex County Council (1990) *Does It Add Up?: National Curriculum Guidelines: Mathematics*. Lewes: East Sussex County Council.

East Sussex County Council (1991) *A Hitchhiker's Guide to Humanities, National Curriculum Guidelines*. Lewes: East Sussex County Council.

Eggleston, J. (1980) 'The drawbacks of projects', *Times Educational Supplement*, 12 September 1980.

Eisner E. (1985) *The Art of Educational Evaluation*. London: Falmer.

Fagg, S., Skelton, S. Aherne, P. and Thornber, A. (1990) *Science for All*. London: Fulton.

Fagg, S. (1991) 'Perspectives on the National Curriculum', In: Ashdown, R., Carpenter, B. and Bovair, K. (eds) *The Curriculum Challenge: Access to the National Curriculum for Pupils with Learning Difficulties*. London: Falmer.

Farrell, P., McBrien, J. and Foxen T. (1992) *EDY Second Edition*. Manchester: Manchester University Press.

Friere, P. (1972) *Pedagogy of the Oppressed*. Harmondsworth: Penguin.

Frostig, M. and Horne, D. (1967) *Handbook to the Frostig Programme of Visual Perception*. Chicago: Follett.

Gleason, J. (1989) *Special Education in Context*. Cambridge: Cambridge University Press.

Gunzberg, H.C. (1968) *Social Competence and Mental Handicap*. London: Bailliere Tindall.

Hamblin, D. (1978) *The Teacher and Pastoral Care*. Oxford: Blackwell.

Hamblin, D. (1981) *Teaching Study Skills*. Oxford: Blackwell.

Hart, S. (1992) 'Differentiation - way forward or retreat?', *British Journal of Special Education*, 19, (1), 10-12.

Hart, S. and Ainscow, M. (1992) 'Moving practice forward', *Support for Learning*, 7, (3), 115-120.

Hewett, D. (1989) 'The most severe learning difficulties: does your curriculum 'go back far enough'?', In: Ainscow, M. (ed) *Special Education in Change*. London: Fulton.

Holly P. and Southworth G. (1989) *The Developing School*. London: Falmer.

Hopkins D. (1985) *A Teachers Guide to Classroom Research*. Oxford: Oxford University Press.

Hughes, N. and Carpenter, B. (1991) 'Annual reviews: an active partnership', In: Ashdown, R., Carpenter, B. and Bovair, K. (eds) *The Curriculum Challenge: Access to the National Curriculum for Pupils with Learning Difficulties*. London: Falmer.

Humberside County Council (1990) *Access to Science for Pupils with Special Educational Needs Key Stages 1 and 2*. Hull: Humberside County Council.

Humberside County Council (1992) *Access to History for Children with Special Educational Needs Key Stages 1-4*. Hull: Humberside County Council.

Johnson, D. W. and Johnson, R.T. (1982) 'The effects of cooperative and individualistic instruction on handicapped and non-handicapped students', *Journal of Social Psychology*, 118, 257-268.

Johnson, D. W. and Johnson, F.P. (1987) *Joining Together: Group Theory and Group Skills*. (Third Edition). Englewood Cliffs, New Jersey: Prentice Hall.

Johnson, D. W., Johnson, R. T. and Johnson-Holubec, E. (1990) *Circles of Learning*. (Third Edition). New Brighton, MN.: Interaction Book Company.

Kephart, N.C. (1971) *The Slow Learner in the Classroom*. Columbus Ohio: Merrill (2nd edition).

Kiernan, C. and Woodford, P. (1975) *Behaviour Modification with the Severely Retarded*. Amsterdam: Associated Scientific Publishers.

Knowles, W. and Masidlover, M. (1982) *The Derbyshire Language Scheme.* Ripley, Derbyshire: Private Publication.

Lawson H. (1992) Practical Record Keeping for Special Schools. London: Fulton.

McBrien, J. and Foxen, T. (1981) *Training Staff in Behavioural Methods: The EDY IN-Service Course for Mental Handicap Practitioners*. Manchester: Manchester University Press.

McCall, C. (1983) *Classroom Grouping for Special Need*. Stratford upon Avon: National Council for Special Education.

McGee, J.J., Menolascino, F.J., Hobbs, D.C. and Menousek, P.E. (1987) *Gentle Teaching - A Non-Aversive Approach to Helping Persons with Mental Retardation*. New York: Human Sciences Press.

McLaughlin, C. (1990) 'Personal and social education - Where and what is it now?', *Cambridge Institute of Education Newsletter*, 16.

Mager, R.F. (1962) *Preparing Instructional Objectives*. Belmont, California: Fearon.

Moon R, and Oliver L. (1985) 'Redefining school concepts of ability - the experience of the LAPP project', *Curriculum*, 6, (3), 40-44.

Mount, H. and Ackerman, D. (1991) *Technology for All*. London: Fulton.

NCC (1989) *Curriculum Guidance 2: A Curriculum for All*. York: NCC.

NCC (1990a) *Curriculum Guidance 3: The Whole Curriculum*. York: NCC.

NCC (1990b) *Curriculum Guidance 4: Education for Economic and Industrial Understanding*. York: NCC.

NCC (1990c) *Curriculum Guidance 5: Health Education*. York: NCC.

NCC (1990d) *Curriculum Guidance 6: Careers Education and Guidance*. York: NCC.

NCC (1990e) *Curriculum Guidance 7: Environmental Education*. York: NCC.

NCC (1990f) *Curriculum Guidance 8: Education for Citizenship*. York: NCC.

NCC (1992a) *Curriculum Guidance 9: The National Curriculum and Pupils with Severe Learning Difficulties*. York: NCC.

NCC (1992b) *The National Curriculum and Pupils with Severe Learning Difficulties: INSET Resources*. York: NCC.

Newman, K. and Rose, R. (1990) 'Self evaluation at Wren Spinney', *British Journal of Special Education*, 17, (1), 12-14.

Nind, M. and Hewett, D. (1988) 'Interaction as curriculum', *British Journal of Special Education*, 15, (2), 55-57.

Ouvry, C. (1991) 'Access for pupils with profound and multiple learning difficulties'. In Ashdown, R., Carpenter, B. and Bovair, K. (eds) *The Curriculum Challenge: Access to the National Curriculum for Pupils with Learning Difficulties*. London: Falmer.

Pring, R. (1984) *Personal and Social Education in the Curriculum*. London: Hodder and Stoughton.

Rectory Paddock School Staff (1983) *In Search of a Curriculum*. Sidcup: Robin Wren Publications.

Reid K., Hopkins D. and Holly P. (1987) *Towards the Effective School*. Oxford: Blackwell.

Rogers, C. (1983) *Freedom to Learn for the 80's*. Columbus, Ohio: Charles E. Merrill Publishing Co.

Rose, R. (1991) 'A jigsaw approach to group work', *British Journal of Special Education*, 18, (2), 54-57.

Ryder, J. and Campbell, L. (1988) *Balancing Acts in Personal, Social and Health Education*. London: Routledge.

Sebba, J. (1988) *The Education of People with Profound and Multiple Handicaps: Resource Material for Staff Training*. Manchester: Manchester University Press.

Sebba J. and Fergusson A. (1991) 'Reducing the marginalisation of pupils with severe learning difficulties through curricular initiatives'. In Ainscow, M. (ed) *Effective Schools For All*. London: Fulton.

Sebba, J., Galloway, S. and Rodbard, G. (1991) *Water: An Integrated Approach for Meeting the Needs of Pupils with Profound and Multiple Learning Difficulties within the National Curriculum: A Resource Pack for Teachers*. Hertford: Hertfordshire County Council.

Sebba, J. and Byers, R. (1992) 'The National Curriculum: control or liberation for pupils with learning difficulties', *The Curriculum Journal*, 3, (1), 143-160.

Sherborne, V. (1990) *Developmental Movement for Children*. Cambridge: Cambridge University Press.

Sheridan, M. (1975) *The Developmental Progress of Infants and Young Children*. London: HMSO.

Skinner, B.F. (1953) *Science and Human Behaviour*. New York: Macmillan.

Skinner, B.F. (1966) 'Operant Behavior', In: Honig, W. K. (ed) *Operant Behavior: Areas of Research and Application*. New York: Appleton Century-Crofts.

Slavin, R. (1987) *Cooperative Learning*. Washington D.C.: National Education Association.

Smith, B. (ed)(1987) *Interactive Approaches to the Education of Children with Severe Learning Difficulties*. Birmingham: Westhill College.

Swann, W. (1992) 'Hardening the hierarchies: the National Curriculum as a system of classification'. In Booth, T., Swann, W., Masterton, M. and Potts, P. (eds) *Learning for All: 1: Curricula for Diversity in Education*. London: Routledge.

Swing, S. and Peterson, P. (1982) 'The relationship of student ability and small group interaction to student achievement', *American Educational Research Journal*, 19, (2), 259-274.

Tann, S. (1988) 'Grouping and the integrated classroom'. In: Thomas, G. and Feiler, A. (eds) *Planning for Special Needs*. Oxford: Basil Blackwell.

Tansley, A. E. and Gulliford, R. (1960) *The Education of Slow Learning Children*. London: Routledge and Kegan Paul.

Thomas, N. (1982) 'Topics in turmoil', *Times Educational Supplement*, 1 October 1982.

Tilstone, C. (ed) (1991) *Teaching Pupils with Severe Learning Difficulties*. London: Fulton.

Wall, W.D. (1974) *Constructive Education for Adolescents*. London: UNESCO/Harrap.

Watkins, C. (1989) *Whole School Policies for Personal-Social Education: the ingredients and the processes*. Warwick: NAPCE.

West M. and Ainscow M. (1991) *Managing School Development: A Practical Guide*. London: Fulton.

Wheldall, K. and Merritt, C. (1984) *BATPACK*. Birmingham: Positive Products.

White, M. and Cameron, R.J. (1987) *Portage Early Education Programme*. Revised, anglicized version. Windsor: NFER-NELSON.

Wood, S. and Shears, B. (1986) *Teaching Children with Severe Learning Difficulties: A Radical Re-appraisal*. London: Croom Helm.

Wragg, T. (1990) 'Time for a fling with the cabinet'. *Times Educational Supplement*, 20 July 1990.

Author Index

Subject Index

106

Risk taking 32.

Schemes of work 92–94.
School development planning 56, 63, 67, 73, 92–3.
Science 16, 20–22, 33, 36, 53, 62.
Self advocacy 79, 93.
Self directed learning 32, 36, 91.
Self help skills 18, 28–9, 76, 78.
Selfhood 78–9.
Seven selves 77–8, 92.
Sex education 19, 76.
SNAP (Special Needs Action Package) 10.
Societal expectations 79–80, 82–3.
Speech therapy 72.
Staff development 63–4, 91–4.
Statutory Assessments 8, 19–20.
Statements 11.
Subject coordinators 62–71.

Teacher/pupil relationships 5, 18, 48, 84–9, 93–4.

power & control 11, 36, 84–8.
partnership 83, 88.
rules, routines & rituals 85–6.
help & guidance 86–7.
hierarchies 87.
praise, reward & punishment 87–8.
Teaching and learning styles 6, 27–55, 75, 77, 83, 91–3.
Teaching packages 9–10.
Technology 16, 32, 36, 53, 62, 68.
Terminology 4–5.
Therapists 4, 18, 22, 57, 72.
Timetabling 67–8, 76, 85.
Topics 31–4, 68.

Warnock Report 7.
Whole curriculum 14–26, 57, 74–8, 80, 89, 93–4.
Whole person education 89–93.
curriculum 91.
casework 91.
control 91.
management 91.